Getting to the Heart

*A Journey of
Soul Transformation
and Spiritual Enlightenment*

Athene Raefiel

Copyright © 2018 by Athene Raefiel.

All rights reserved. No part of this publication may be reproduced, distributed, or transmitted in any form or by any means, including photocopying, recording, or other electronic or mechanical methods, without the prior written permission of the author, except in the case of brief quotations embodied in critical reviews and certain other noncommercial uses permitted by copyright law.

Excerpts may be copied and used from this book with Athene Raefiel acknowledged as the Author.

First Edition ¾ 1998
Updated, Revised and Expanded edition ¾ 2002
Reprint edition 2018

Cover design by Sharon George
Gorgeous George Graphics
www.gorgeousgeorge.com

Edited by Athene Raefiel

Printed in the United States of America

ISBN: 978-1-949362-37-4 (Paperback)
ISBN: 978-1-949362-36-7 (eBook)

Library of Congress Control Number: 2018953010

Stonewall Press
363 Paladium Court
Owings Mills, MD 21117
www.stonewallpress.com
1-888-334-0980

Also by the author:

Guided Channeled Meditation CDs
Enhancing the Teachings of this Book:

The Sacred Garden & The Sacred Circle

Stairway of Angels & The Halls of Learning

Inner Child Meditation

Anchoring Light, Creating Sacred Space, Prayers for the Planet

CD's can be found at CD baby.com
www.atheneraefiel.com

Contents

Acknowledgments vii
Message from the Author ix

PART I - UNDERSTANDING SOUL

Getting to the Heart 3
The Soul's Journey 8
The Astral Plane 13
The Child Within 16
Letting Go 19
Our Conditioning 22
The Spiritual Quest Begins 25
Changing Realities 30
Morality and Religion 34
Meditation 38
Initiation 42
Self-realization 47
Enlightenment 51

PART II - WORKBOOK

The Workbook 57
Creating a Sacred Space 59
Invocations and prayers 64
Invocation to the Holy Light Within 66
What is processing? 67
What are Chakras 81
Forgiveness 89
Affirmations 100
Create Your Own Affirmations 105
Self-Dialogue 107
Visualization: *A Key to Awareness* 116

About the Author 126
Suggested Reading 128
Glossary 130

ACKNOWLEDGMENTS

I thank my loving husband, Bill King, for his great faith in me and for his loving patience and support. The balance Bill brings into my life allows me to stay grounded long enough to bring words to paper while juggling a personal and business life.

I acknowledge my friend Barb Taylor, who has always believed in my work and assisted me continually.

I also thank all my friends; students, family, and clients, who have supported and acknowledged my gifts and abilities helping me to find the faith necessary to move forward with my many projects.

In addition, most importantly, I thank my companions in spirit, who continually inspire me through their great love and compassion for humankind.

Message from the Author

We are entering a time of great-accelerated growth and development as a planet and a species. Tides are changing and earth changes amass. Daily living has become stressed and personal identity is no longer easy to define. We are shifting into a time of great spiritual conception.

We are no longer living in harmony with the earth or one another. We can no longer pretend everything is all right when it is not. No longer can we deny our own soul and spirit essence if we are to sustain life upon this earth, our homeland.

This is not a book of doom and gloom but one of understanding how to restore the love and harmony needed to renew us, to renew the planet. We are all part of the greater life plan; all we need do to fulfill our part is to recognize it. The roles of life that we have been playing are of no important consequence when not played in conjunction with the divine role.

In order for us to recognize ourselves as being mind, body and spirit, we need tools for change and evolvement. Taking the initiative to become aware of all the aspects of life and self will aid in each person's development. Whether you are just beginning or already advanced, this book shares insights and tools for all to create a better more fulfilled life.

As we begin to open our minds and our hearts, we find that the meaning of life has not really been hidden from us but simply covered up. We discover within us the ability to perceive what we thought to be impossible, thereby allowing light to shine into our lives. This is the only role in life that the Divine requests of us in order for us to fulfill our destiny. It is a simple role yet so few truly seek to achieve this task.

We need to open ourselves to the process of discovery and quit thinking that we know everything. The only true knowing that exists is that there is always more to learn and discover.

Each of us are a Universe unto ourselves, as such we are infinite. This being true, self-discovery goes on ad infinitum.

Become an explorer as you read and use this book. Allow yourself to glean a new array of gems discovering pearls of wisdom as you open to enlightenment. Let this book become a friend that shares with you a new way of seeing yourself; a friend you go to in time of need and comfort. A friend that offers you tools for changing old belief patterns and worn out behaviors. With the aid of your new friend you will discover that there are momentous treasures buried within you offering true means of empowerment.

Athene Raefiel

PART I - UNDERSTANDING SOUL

Getting to the Heart

There are many beings spiritually awakening on the planet at this time. As one awakens and chooses to follow their spiritual path and open to the Universe, they can find themselves besieged with obstacles and hardship. This occurs because of unresolved issues in present and past incarnations.

Spiritual development—the soul's journey—can only be attained and understood by developing ones spirit consciousness. Spirit consciousness is not the ability to speak with spirits but to understand how we ourselves are spirits.

Opening the third eye is a major step in our spiritual development. The third eye is the chakra center of clairvoyance and clairaudience in the auric field. When the third eye center becomes activated, we experience what is called inner dimensional seeing and hearing. With the activation of this chakra comes visions and new body sensations.

Using the third eye can greatly enhance your intuitive nature but cannot, by itself, heal your life. The other six major energy centers in your auric field must be activated and developed as well. The most important of these major centers is the heart chakra.

A chakra center is a spiraling vortex, or wheel of light, located in every auric field of energy. All living things are surrounded with an auric field. This field is the life-giving force for all evolutionary processes.

Each human being has an auric field that contains seven major chakra centers and twenty-one minor chakra centers. The chakra centers within every human auric field are interconnected but only become activated and utilized through our need and freewill choice.

The chakra system, when seen in the auric field is aligned with the physical body along the spinal column.

These energy "wheels of light" appear at the base of the spine, the sacral area, the navel, the heart, the throat, in the center of the brow just above the eyes, and atop the head at the crown, where the soft spot was when we were born. (See diagram on page 81.)

The chakra centers that are activated and used daily are the root chakra, the sacral chakra, and the solar plexus. These three are referred to as the lower chakra centers. They are connected to our instinct to survive. For us to be able to think, feel, or eat on our own, their use is mandatory in our day to day living. We develop our conditioned responses to others and to life through these chakras.

The fourth chakra, the heart center, is activated and utilized through the experience of unconditional love. Unconditional love is when we love without expectation or need. Often as babies and young children, we felt this unconditional love from our parents and others. By receiving love in this manner, we naturally responded unconditionally.

When we are born, we are born into a life where conditioned responses and feelings are developed and learned. Yet, we are born with our DNA already encoded with the life lessons we need to learn. This encoding happens when the soul enters the body. The conditions we experience in any given lifetime are already preprogrammed through our previous incarnation's karma.

The upper three chakras–the throat, brow, and crown–are known as our spiritual chakra centers, when these energy centers are activated and employed, we are in touch with our eternal or soul essence.

The heart chakra is the center in your energetic body that balances the upper and lower chakras. This chakra is the bridge between the physical and spiritual worlds of understanding and awareness. Both the spirit and physical worlds being consciousness, the heart center balances the animal and humane nature or our conditional and unconditional love.

The workings of the heart chakra can be equated to the workings of the physical heart. The physical heart has many chambers and each chamber must work properly for the heart to be fully healthy. The heart pumps blood through every vital organ in the body; it is our lifeline. If any vessel leading to or from the heart is constricted or blocked, the body no longer works as a whole organism. So it is with the heart chakra.

In order for the heart chakra to operate properly, it must be maintained to remain clear and flowing. If within this energy center we store distorted beliefs that we have acquired through our many learning experiences, we in essence block the flow of unconditional love and deny ourselves the experience of true spirituality. It is only by examining and healing our beliefs from past experiences that we begin to open ourselves to our inner divine awareness.

Too often, our past memories of pain, betrayal, disappointment, and loss stop us from truly exploring our heart and its many mysteries. It is often easier to believe that spiritual salvation comes in the form of a savior or a psychic connection than to accept responsibility for our own salvation. In truth, it is at the very core of the heart that each person's true nature lies. The nature of how they are the *spirit within.*

When we allow our self to make the connection to our spirit essence, positive life changes can begin manifesting. Spiritual enlightenment now becomes the primary destination and the quest for integration of mind, body and spirit ensues. Ones key life experiences can now be realized, allowing happiness to replace complacency; love to replace need and acceptance to replace control.

When we truly live our life from the heart, realizations take place within the whole being and we simply begin to understand inner truth. Experiencing ourselves in this manner opens us to a means of resolution to problems that have daunted us throughout our lives.

When we have realizations in this manner, answers become apparent within the different dimensions of self, thus creating a powerful sense of knowing. At first these realizations may seem to have no rational explanation, yet they continually bring an understanding that assists us in feeling differently about our environment and ourselves.

To truly see something multidimensionally, one must become multidimensional. This can only be accomplished by discovering who *one* is on the inside. What is on the inside cannot be seen but must be experienced to be realized. This can only occur by using and developing our sense perception.

Although we have developed our outer senses of touch, sight, hearing, smell, and taste, we still must develop the inner senses of sensitivity. The inner senses are imperative to our spiritual survival just as the outer are to our physical survival.

A true spiritual teacher, healer, or psychic needs to become spiritually integrated in order to serve the greater good of all. When one can finally walk in truth and light of their inner being, they no longer feel a need to put on airs or seek the approval of others.

Our creators designed us to be multidimensional beings. We are designed in "their own image", and they are multidimensional. We need only to remember and become aware of ourselves dimensionally while in the human experience to understand this concept. If you believe in life after death, then you must understand that life on the other side is simply an extension of this one. In death we simply de-robe the physical body and step into a different dimension of self. There truly is no end in death, only new and different experiences for our soul progression and evolution.

What we need to learn and understand is that we do not need to die to be saved. Our physical body need not die for us to experience spiritual growth and transformation. We can transition and open to the innermost chambers of our heart and become aware of the energy beings we are right here and now.

THE SOUL'S JOURNEY

As the quest for discovering soul begins we turn our senses inward to discover our true path of enlightenment. As we make our journey, we will find many books, tapes, seminars and teachers available to guide us on our wonderful exploration. Wise sages and great mystic teachers of old and new have always, and still do, profess the importance of *the inner journey*. Like all things that hold great rewards, accessing our soul awareness is no small task and must be taken on with diligence and perseverance.

The soul's operation is unique in its process of evolution. Much like a computer, our soul stores information for future reference. Our soul is a memory container filled with information of all that was, is, and will be in life. Since all information is contained within the soul, from the very personal to the collective whole, when one re-enters their soul awareness, they are able to access this multitude of data.

Soul travel is experienced through the exploration of consciousness. Each chakra center emits an invisible body through which consciousness is experienced. The consciousness body of the heart chakra is sometimes known as the astral body. It is through this astral body of consciousness that we are able to travel within the soul. When the heart chakra is not cleansed and purified of the past debris imprisoning it, we are not able to truly understand our soul self.

The soul is the vehicle through which we connect with our spirit essence. It is within soul that we remember whom we are as spirit and realign ourselves to that awareness.

The soul is often referred to as the Christ Consciousness. When Jesus Christ walked the earth and shared the great mystery teachings of the cosmos, he made the fact of the soul quite clear, by espousing to be, "The Way, The Truth, and The Light." He came as Jesus the Christ consciousness, or the soul of humanity, not Jesus the human person as so many believed. Jesus Christ was only one of the many mystic teachers to bring us spiritual awareness and understanding. Hermes, Krishna, Moses, Orpheus, and Plato also taught great spiritual truths as well as many others.

The intermediate state one passes through to attain spirit awareness is known as Christ consciousness. Many other faiths such as Buddhism, Brahmanism, Hinduism, Judaism, all have their initiations for this process.

Once one becomes immersed in a study of spiritual enlightenment, the appetite for learning often becomes ravenous. This is very natural, as human nature can be insatiable. It is important that we not try to move beyond that which we need to learn the most. Though the thirst for knowledge and awareness may be great, we can not skip steps when trying to attain understanding of the cosmic self.

Our heart chakra is our connection to our soul and our spirit awakening. Our soul is our connection of physical and spiritual attunement. The soul journey of awareness is mandatory to attain spiritual enlightenment. Many think that scholarly learning brings enlightenment. When learning of the inner self there is only so much you can learn through reading. The rest must be experienced.

When learning to go within, the intuitive self becomes the instrument of learning. Often we discover that the rational mind becomes an obstacle when developing intuitively. Trial and error is how we learn.

As we awaken to our fourth dimensional consciousness, or *soul awareness*, we experience a feeling of rebirth. It sometimes feels as if we are awakening from a deep sleep to discover that we have missed a whole scope of what's been going on around and within us. Upon reaching this great transitory point we need to develop patience and take the time to explore and thoroughly learn about the New World we are re-entering.

This is an exciting time of discovery but may be somewhat draining at first. It is like starting a new workout program. When activating something within you that has been lying around a lot, it takes some exertion to re-establish proper flow and usage to get it operational again.

Our human nature always pushes us to try to move beyond that which we are doing in the moment. Too often, people wish to jump ahead to fifth dimensional awareness before fully exploring the fourth. This is like trying to advance to college before learning to read and write, or trying to roller-skate before learning to walk. Know always that there is an order to the Universe, and we are all part of that order. This same *universe* orders all learning and the movement through different levels of consciousness. There is no learning beyond the place that you are; the universe that you are is already ordered and prepared for the correct steps. Reel in your impatience and allow yourself to surrender to the moment. Realize that time exists only in your mind. Inner reality is timeless.

The Soul Matrix

Within the soul dwells darkness and light, ignorance and enlightenment, pain and joy. The ignorant or dark part of the soul has no awareness of the unconditional life that awaits. It has no remembrance of unconditional love. Everything within the dark part of the soul feeds itself from the conditional being. Beliefs that are anchored in the dark part of the soul have been handed down from generation to generation and accepted as truth. These beliefs are powerful and are rooted in ignorance. People who live by and teach such beliefs have allowed the veil between the dark and light of the soul to become a wall, a barrier that separates them from their spiritual awareness of self. People dwelling in this darkness have accepted despair, hatred, pain, and ignorance to be their life. They have created a reality for themselves that is a living hell and they continually share and teach this reality to others. On the wheel of karma, one experiences what one believes until a new reality is created. Hence, one can experience many lifetimes within this reality, before awakening to the light within their soul.

By opening and clearing the emotional debris from within the heart chakra, we begin connecting through our soul's matrix. All souls contain this matrix.

If we could see the soul, its appearance is like that of our DNA. The American Heritage Dictionary defines DNA as "a polymeric chromosomal constituent of living cell nuclei."

Our individual souls form strands that look like two long chains twisted into a double helix.

All souls work within soul groups. There are many millions of souls within each soul group, and each soul group is an oversoul and also has an oversoul.

When a group of souls has completed the experiential journey necessary for the stages of their current growth and development, they evolve through the soul matrix into the next soul group. This is known as the ascension process. This process takes place within each soul group throughout many eons of time. We ascend the ladder of soul evolution by experiencing first unconsciously, then consciously.

Our group oversoul is comprised of spiritual beings that have moved beyond the need for the human body experience. In metaphysics they are called Ascended Masters. We refer to them as such, because they have mastered human life and its many trials. They themselves, following the journey of soul evolution have now become pure divine beings.

Ascension is the process to which we adhere for the awareness of alternate consciousness. The ascension process is achieved through integrating all of our awareness understood thus far. This can be done on a daily basis, thereby allowing us a degree of continual ascension.

All souls are interconnected through their soul matrix. When you open your heart self to your divine awareness, you automatically connect with divine oversoul. Divine oversoul can now assist you in breaking free of the conditioned, troubled dark part of the soul that continually struggles to survive in chaos. The journey may seem arduous at times, yet when we connect with the light of the soul we clearly see how stuck we have been in the darkness.

At first it may sometimes feel overwhelming to glimpse the amount of work there is to be done on yourself, but clarity brings it's own rewards. As it is with all good things in life, the love, and support we now need also makes itself available to us.

The Astral Plane

Within the astral plane are many different levels of existence. When we remember that the heart chakra is attached to both the upper and lower chakras, exploration of the astral becomes one of a spiritual as well as physical nature. All things being interconnected and part of a whole, whatever people believe to be truth, is created and dwells within the astral plane. The astral body and astral consciousness experientially travel throughout the astral plane continually. In the physical plane, we, our planet and solar system are all within the astral plane.

The astral is a repository of the energies of the Cosmos on their way downwards and it is a receptacle of whatever passes out of the physical sphere on its way upward.

Exploring the astral plane is like going to a library that is filled with an immense variety of categories and experiences. Each person's book of life as well as all the stories of creation is catalogued within the astral library.

All information and learning in the astral is transmitted and received through a process of osmosis. In this manner, we actually absorb information though our inner awareness and understanding.

In metaphysics, the astral library is often referred to as the Akashic Records. To understand fully the volumes of information we have access to here; we need to become spiritually integrated. The five outer senses are of little use when exploring the astral plane and Akashic records; opening and developing the inner senses is primary.

One of the levels of experience within the astral plane is referred to by some as hell, or purgatory. This dimension is where the so-called demons reside.

Every thought and emotion humankind experiences produce energy. Through our fears and vivid imaginations, we create energies that often produce entities. These thought forms dwell within the astral plane and are seen as demons. Not all demons are bad. Many religions refer to Angels and other beings of light as being demons as well. Yet energies that are created from ignorance and fear are dark energies and feed off the negative emotions of man. Needing negative emotion to survive they often attack humans in their sleeping and waking state producing fear and hatred so as to feed. Hence came the lore of vampires.

Seemingly, human beings cannot make themselves do what is good unless they have the threat of evil to overcome. This martyr program has been taught as a religious dogma helping humans acquiesce to it as being their nature. The power of evil is great only because of the power we give it.

Energy creates, and beliefs are very potent energies. When people believe in fear, pain, chaos, and deprivation, these projected energies take on a form and life of their own.

The dwelling place of these vampire energies is known as the lower astral. These are our energies; therefore, they become our demons. When we die, these entities remain in the lower astral awaiting our return to earth. When we reincarnate, these energies are restored to us because we are their creators and only we have the power to un-create them.

We must see for our self what we have initially created, before we can create anew. Because all things are created from energy, all things can be brought back to a pure energy state. Reacting in fear or ignorance when confronted with these creations blocks our spiritual progression. By continual denial of the existence of these blocks humans remain stagnate and remain stuck in dysfunction.

When we open our hearts to transmute our creations, "our demons", they disappear. This only happens by us bringing them a pure energy state of love. Love is the eternal fire of life that burns within every heart. Love is the greatest healer that we have.

THE HIGHER ASTRAL

Heavenly worlds of color and geometry also dwell in the astral plane, awaiting exploration. Using astral consciousness, one can see and experience Angels and Teachers of Light. These beings use this plane of consciousness, to make themselves visible to us.

Using our astral consciousness, we can visit other universes, galaxies, and beautiful temples of love. The astral plane was created for us to have direct accessibility to our companions in spirit. These beings are known as spirit guides. These guides and teachers of love are part of our spiritual family. They are always with us in spirit helping us understand the spiritual nature of our earthly journey.

When people first begin consciously journeying within the astral plane, they tend to doubt the reality of their experiences, suggesting to themselves that its all imagination. They find it inconceivable that such a glorious and magical life can exist in the midst of our chaotic everyday existence.

It is the outer world senses and learned responses that are at first difficult to override. It takes time and training to experience and accept the different realities that exist, especially when they exist within you. Our perceptions can only change when we open and allow it to happen. When we take the time to explore the astral realm, we can discover a limitless multitude of spirit awareness and personal understanding.

The Child Within

We are multi-aspected beings. What this means is that we are always an adult as well as a child, a teacher, a student, a spirit, a soul, a body and so on. If we were stunted emotionally by childhood experiences, we find ourselves re-living those experiences continually throughout life. Most families are comprised of adults whose reality is an," accepted fear for survival". When raised in such an environment children experience a life filled with fear and attachment as a way of surviving.

When a person is brought up in an environment of denial and pain, they stuff their child-like emotions into the deep inner recesses of their being. These things often happen at very early ages and stages of life without us ever even knowing it took place.

Freeing these repressed child-like emotions is key to the soul's journey. As it says in the Bible, "Ye may not enter into the Kingdom of My Father lest ye come as a child", refers to this emotional internal freedom. This child within us is our unconditional loving part. Like a child who has been abandoned by a parent, the *child within* anxiously awaits our return.

Because the *child within* has been damaged through its life experiences involving family and environment, our first memories and responses to it may be painful. Emotions of anger, resentment, hurt, even rage, can be covering the deep love within.

Sometimes when these emotions re-surface the instinct to re-stuff the *child within* may be strong, yet the *child within* holds the key to emotional freedom. All the pain that has been held inside must be released. Once you have reintroduced yourself to your *child within*, the true healing of self can begin.

For all of us, the *child within* is at the heart things. It represents our unconditional understanding and inner divinity. Healing and opening ourselves to learn as a child again, allows us to use the wisdom and experience gained by becoming an adult. Our *child within* assists us in a process of learning anew. We can now parent our *child within*, by sharing, nurturing, loving and accepting him/her. By establishing a new way of development for our inner child, we can create a new bond of trust and hope for the future.

As you get to know your *child within*, you may begin to realize just how fragmented you have become. You will discover that your *child within* has many aspects to be explored. Your inner child may even be a child guide and companion helping you on your path of discovery.

As you begin allowing the *child within* to be your guide, while discovering additional child like emotions buried inside, you discover whole other parts of the emotional body you have suppressed. These emotions represent distinct stages of growth and development in life when emotional development was stunted.

We discover that we become emotionally stuck, because as children we do not have the tools to understand and resolve our dilemmas. As long as the *child within* is imprisoned, we will continue to face the same emotional dilemmas in life as we have in the past.

Freeing and healing the *child within* allows us to change and understand others and ourselves emotionally. The consciousness of the emotional body is connected through our sacral chakra. Through the cleansing and healing of our emotional body, we elevate our emotional vibrations to a heart-felt energy level and transmute the pain of the past. We reinstate the *child within* to our heart chakra where it can grow and dwell in a place of joy and peace.

Letting Go

Letting go does not mean to push away or suppress. True letting go is a process of integration and healing.

Letting go can be a misleading statement because it gives the impression of separation. By integrating a situation that involves you, another person, or a circumstance in life, means to come to terms with it. We can only come to terms with something when we understand it.

When we understand the purpose of our life experiences, we are able to accept them; thereby releasing our emotional attachment. Learning to embrace our issues in this way allows us to take them within ourselves and integrate them.

Once our emotions are understood and integrated our judgments about ourselves and others begin to dissolve. Where there is clarity and understanding, problems cannot germinate.

What we see on the outside of ourselves is a reflection of what is happening on the inside. Interacting with others is always a way of interacting with oneself. When interaction brings up feelings within us that we do not like, we should search inside to see why this is occurring. We should view others in our lives as our mirrors.

Many people create emotional isolation by distancing themselves from others. Using the outside as a reflection of the inside, finding ourselves isolated and disoriented shows us how we are feeling on the inside.

Understanding that the only real problem in your life is *you*, allows you to realize the truth of who you are. Only through thorough self-examination can emotions and feelings be healed. This is true problem solving.

Our accepted beliefs, habits and behaviors—our inner walls—all play a part in who we are. Take for example the critical part of self, who loves to run rampant. This part continually judges and criticizes self and others. This kind of behavior is very often quite destructive. This behavior leads to an out-of-balance, superhuman, perfectionist complex.

It seems to have become the norm to single out what is imperfect about another or oneself rather than identifying what is unique and special. This commonly leads to pettiness and competition, disrespect and dishonor.

We can require that others honor us in the same way that we honor our self, only by treating them as we wish to be treated. We find it is much easier to accept others when we like and accept ourselves. Being critical and judgmental are roadblocks in the path of learning to love.

As we become honest with ourselves and reflect our own attitudes and actions, we see the mirrors that others play in our life.

In understanding why we feel the way we do about our past, we begin to let go. By transmuting pain and sadness into love, we become loving. By changing how we think and view life, we become open-minded. Realizing that one can only change his or herself rather than the world around them alleviates the stress of what you cannot do.

Letting go is the process of fully accepting something as it is with no need to change it. Only through a spiritual perception can we understand the issues faced in life and come to terms with them. Openly embracing life and its lessons with an open and loving heart allows this new perception to emerge within us. This is letting go.

We must be able to forgive and accept our mistakes before we can change them. Embracing with love always brings about the desired change. This is the universal paradox upon which all life is based.

Our Conditioning

We are all products of our environments, our ancestry, our society, and of history. All these things have created the program within us that determines how we live our lives.

When we begin to examine the accepted programs that our personality has accepted a self, we find that little if any of it makes sense. We recognize how we too are the same as our mothers and fathers, our jobs, our children, etc. We realize that we have very little individual identity apart from these things. The current identity we are experiencing was developed to survive our daily life in a very basic manner.

As we seek to understand the deeper meaning of our life and ourselves, we peel off the layers of our survival conditioning to discover what lies beneath the surface. Our conditional self is the surface layer of who we are. The "tip of the iceberg" if you will.

By peeling away the outer conditions of ourselves, we can begin a new quest for knowledge and awareness. Here is where we begin the journey of discovering our spiritual essence. Many people find the "peeling away" process difficult at first; however, to move forward, we first must be able to first identify what holds us in place.

Human conditioning is powerful and we have accepted certain beliefs as being truth for centuries, perhaps even eons of time. We have lived our lives for the elements of pleasure and pain, continually unaware of any other way; when it is suggested that a truer self lies somewhere within us, our conditioning rebels.

Our rational minds and emotional bodies impose doubt and fear of the unknown.

We are taught and believe that it is natural to be afraid of learning more about ourselves.

Is it natural to live only in the experiences of the past, trapped by fear, guilt, anger, and shame? Our conditioning would have us believe this is the way because it knows of no other. It is in this way that the conditioned self becomes stubborn, set in its ways, and stuck in ignorance.

When we seek to know ourselves as spirit, we do so by removing our outer covering and finding what lies underneath. By exploring our hidden depths, we begin to loosen the bonds that have trapped us in the past.

We now see that our personality conditions, our patterns, have to do with gaining the acceptance and approval of others. The good girl or boy our parents wanted us to be, the well-behaved student who got good grades, the wife or husband who lives to make their spouse happy, the employee who is loyal and works overtime without complaint. These are only a few of the many facades and roles we play in life. These facades are the layers through which we must process to find the jewel that lies hidden within—the unconditional spirit self.

When we begin peeling the layers away, it is often difficult to understand how to move beyond our current belief structure. Unconditionally accepting ourself is no small feat. If you want to believe in yourself as spirit and love, you can consciously choose to do so. By acquiring and using the proper tools and with application you will succeed. Nothing less than

Perseverance and dedication are required. To change belief patterns is a continual task. You need be willing to make the effort and take the time.

To begin believing differently, we must open ourselves to our feelings of vulnerability. This allows us to trust in love and to explore the pain that lies within. This initial step is difficult and challenging at first, yet to achieve want we want in life we must take risks. Fear is simply an instinct to survive. If we permit fear to determine who we are then we will never know ourselves as spirit.

The greatest conditioned fear within, is the fear of change. If we are afraid that we are not whom we think we are, then we have no identity to attach to. This fear is so paralyzing that we do not chance to embrace change. Yet change is and always has been the only constant in life. We are all designed to be *changelings*. Believing any other way is illusionary. When we live in the illusion we have created, calling it life, without knowing the eternal essence within; we do not really live, we merely exist.

Learned responses are powerful because we believe in them. When we begin to detach from the energy we have given to our conditioned responses as being truth, they fade.

Our personal reality is completely based on what we believe; when we discover that truth is ever expansive and undeniable, our reality changes. When this transpires, we embark upon the profound and limitless journey within.

The Spiritual Quest Begins

Our three lower chakras represent all the conditioning and attachments developed in life. While developing through the lower chakras we experience only through the carnal nature which is our need to survive. At this stage, the acceptance and approval of others is how we determine our successes and failures in life. The love we learn about through the lower chakras is *a need to be needed.*

Pain and suffering bring about growth and development making them major components of survival. Because like attracts like, we are continually attracting others to ourselves who feel and believe the same way we do. It is only through such experiences that we learn how to change and overcome the past. When stuck in a conditional state of awareness life lessons are experienced continuously. It may be a different time, a different place, or individuals with different faces, yet the lessons are the same. This type of cyclical experience often brings about feelings of helplessness, hopelessness, depression and despondency.

When we begin using and developing the upper chakras, we awaken spiritually. We now discover there is more to life than simply going through the day to day motions. Removing the invisible blindfold from our eyes, though hazy at first, a new picture begins to unfold. Feelings now emerge, signaling us that something very important has been missing in our life. We feel as if we have been under a spell that has now been broken and we are free to explore life in a new way. A new day dawns as we realize that the inner self has been asleep for a very long time. As we stretch and yawn, we may begin to notice a feeling of emptiness inside. Often an intense inner feeling of "wanting to go home" surfaces and we realize that it is the home inside that we are seeking, the center of life and light within that we are.

At first, these stirrings seem a bit foreign. We may feel like strangers in a strange land. A feeling of vulnerability creeps in as our instinct to survive struggles to control, always warning of dangers lurking in the unknown.

Because our conditional self is entering uncharted territory, the awakening self and the survival self suddenly seem to be at odds. The newly awakened spiritual part of us has not had a chance to develop, where as the conditional self already has very strong ingrained beliefs. The new self is fragile and volatile, while the more established instinct to survive *insists* on dominating.

For some, the battle already is over. The memory of the past, of how hard it is to change, dominates and they immediately succumb to their old ways of being. The change necessary to explore the new self seems too costly so they surrender to the dominant—their old dysfunctional comfort zone.

For others, self-realization has been long awaited and no matter what obstacles change may hold, they know it is time to explore the new dimensional reality within. Gathering all the inner strength they can muster, they forge ahead with great determination and perseverance.

The self contains all the answers and awareness of the inner enlightenment we seek. The journey of enlightenment is always about the Self. All one needs do, is find and develop the tools necessary to tap the inner self and discover the spiritual being within.

It is easiest to begin by seeking out self-help books and learning techniques of concentration and contemplation.

Reading everything you can get your hands on that interests you spiritually will open many doors.

Visualization and meditation practices help you control the mind while also exploring it. Using visualization exercises, facilitates the inner journey- work and can prove invaluable as an everyday tool. There are multitudes of books and tapes, both video and audio, that can assist in guiding your exploration.

Regression therapy is another tool that can be valuable in spiritual development. With a spiritual regressionist, you can explore your past, your childhood and even other lives while healing into your spiritual essence.

In a regressed state, you enter a relaxed safe place that allows you to identify the patterns and conditions holding you in place. These conditions are emotional blocks that need to be healed for you to re-open your unconditional loving self. Through regression, you can easily see and understand why you think and feel the way you do. Here you find you are able to heal and change many of the dysfunctional patterns stuck in your emotional and mental bodies. With this process, you can learn to see and understand how the patterns within you have developed.

Hypnosis (regression therapy) also allows you to explore past lives. Here you can trace a problem or pattern that helps you determine other factors involving conditions this lifetime. Regression therapy can produce profound results when done correctly.

When searching for a hypnotherapist, look for someone who has undergone the various procedures he or she plans to take you through. Look for someone with transpersonal training that is in touch with his or her own spirituality. Find out about the person's years of experience and what regression therapy has brought about for them in their life. Do not be afraid to ask questions that will add to your feeling of safety and comfort. As with any physician or therapist they are all different, so ask about applied techniques and past case results.

Meditation, visualization, and regression therapy are very powerful tools to strengthen and activate the four upper chakra centers in your body. Using meditation to go into trance is worthwhile because it helps you develop access to your soul and unconscious mind.

In a trance state, you begin to activate and use your third-eye chakra. This center is used to balance the hemispheres of the left and right brain bringing about inner-dimensional vision. Once the left and right brains are balanced, your crown chakra begins its activation. Now you are opening your unconscious mind and tapping soul memory. Once you achieve this, an entire new element of memory begins to emerge. It is as if a storage compartment in the brain opens up that you never even knew you had. The changes you experience are subtle yet profound.

At this juncture, people often begin remembering their dreams and describe them as being in color. There is a heightened awareness of the senses both inside and out. A feeling of peace often pervades. The feeling self again becomes an active participant in daily life.

Self-healing work can feel a bit overwhelming at times, but in understanding that your conditions and patterns were developed over time helps you understand that it will take time to change and heal. This is a new learning process you have embarked upon, so be patient with the process and yourself.

This day and age we all want instant results, quick fixes, and magic medicine that works overnight. We know intuitively there is no quick cure for a long-standing disease, yet we want instantaneous results.

The physical body's process for healing itself is time and patience. It is the same for the subtle bodies in our energy field. The emotional and mental bodies contain long standing ingrained patterning that may have taken lifetimes to come about. We must give them the proper attention in order to heal them.

The rewards and self-gratification achieved from our inner work are greater than anyone can imagine. Doing inner healing work on a regular basis truly brings miraculous changes into our personal life. These changes can give us peace of mind and true security for the future.

As you explore your inner spiritual nature, your priorities and outlook will begin to change. Your previous beliefs will simply not hold the same importance as they did before. The vessel you are now becoming prepares itself to empty the old so it may be filled with the new. Cleansing and releasing the inner debris of your past perceptions allows you to begin changing your life.

We sometimes feel void or empty inside while this is occurring, but we can only see the light that resides within when we are empty of the debris that blinds us.

This part of the process is referred to as the "peeling off of layers". As you slough off your outer casing, like peeling an apple, you get to the sweetness that lies within. If you have never concentrated on yourself or your life in this way before, initiating such an undertaking may seem astronomical. Remember to be patient. The first mountain you climb will be the most difficult.

Ah yes, the light within! The light is what we all are searching for. That spark within us that ignites the flame of God that we are. This is the path we travel to return home to our home of origin, our divinity. When we are in our light, we are anchored within the center of all life; here we are one with Source. Being centered in this manner allows us the freedom to be who we truly are without conditional attachment.

Upon entering the light, we become illumined. In illumination we find clarity, and with clarity we achieve understanding and wisdom. Only now can we understand and accept our life lessons with renewed awareness. We can now allow, what we once perceived to be obstacles, to instead be our teacher. This shows us how to experience a life of joy and aspiration.

CHANGING REALITIES

When we are stuck in survival, we are convinced there is no time for spirituality. Humankind refuses to explore its eternal essence because there is comfort in believing that logic and reason are the keys to life. This denial of the spirit self has brought our species to a point in our development that is causing self-destruction.

Through this process of denial, humanity has created a world that dwells in torment and debris. The garbage keeps piling up, the atmosphere is unhealthy, trees and vegetation are dying and the destruction is continual. Humans close their eyes constantly to the pain and suffering around them, just as they shut themselves off from their emotions. In the West we call ourselves civilized and worship technology as our savior. Our life has become one of entertainment and drama rather than intimate loving interaction. Most of humanity lives in an illusionary field of dreams that has become a living hell, a world where hope and love are as fleeting thoughts and greed is the great taskmaster.

When we begin to look beyond the veil of illusion, we realize that humanity is on a collision course with its true destiny. To save the world and its inhabitants, we must first learn to save ourselves. Before we can do selfless acts of kindness, we must first learn how to be selfless. This we can only learn by honoring our spiritual essence.

In the spirit realms, all is comprised of energy. Energy continually replenishes itself, ever transforming and changing. This life-giving energy is unending, all-pervading and always exchanging within itself.

You and I are this same spiritual energy. As such, we are learning to change and transform ourselves as energy does. When stuck in the experiences of the lower chakras, our need to survive supersedes the awareness and understanding of ourselves as soul and spirit. Because of this we have become cut off from our spirit self, the energy self that we are.

Our soul can receive sustenance only by us connecting with our spiritual energy. Our soul is our transportation within all consciousness through all incarnations, be they physical or spiritual. We in essence kill ourselves to our soul by denying it the energy exchange it needs.

In reality, the soul cannot die, but we can separate ourselves from our soul memory and consciousness. Doing this creates a barrier that makes it harder and harder to return to soul. When this continues over extended periods, we lose touch with our life-sustaining spiritual energy and we feel devoid and disconnected from life. We become as ghouls and our bodies and minds begin to shut down.

The reality now taking place on planet earth has taken eons of time to establish. Humankind has been shutting itself down for a long time. The societies of this world facilitate this desecration of life and this current existence has now been accepted as true reality. Though many of us would like to see this change overnight, the only way that could happen, is if the majority of people on the planet would actually work through all their lifetimes of conditioning. Changing the conditions of one person's life takes time. How much time will it take for everyone on the planet to realize that we all should seek to become spiritually aware?

By focusing on our individual roles, we will not allow ourselves to be overwhelmed by the vastness of the work that lies ahead. Finding the truth within all life and ourselves is the key.

The spiritual journey should not be taken on half-heartedly. We cannot learn a little and think that is enough. We must persevere---even in the face of crises and adversity, realizing that in some way we too are responsible for the state of affairs the world is in.

Developing through the soul's awareness helps us to perceive and understand the meanings of events in life without attachment. When we are attached to outcome, we still have personal expectations that set us up for disappointment. When we release expectation, we use our inner knowing to take us forward in the creative process of living.

Each person has been born to accept and learn about him or herself as a divine being. Each person is born with unconditional love, compassion, awareness and understanding. It is through our life experiences that we learn to forget this.

Some of you may be asking if it is really necessary to go through all this hoopla of meditation, forgiveness and so forth to develop and open spiritually. Is this awareness attainable in any other fashion?

The answer is simply no. Unless we develop conscious awareness of our multidimensional-self transcending and ascension are not possible.

Meditation, affirmations, purposeful emotional release processes, and meditative trance are tools for deprogramming accepted belief patterns. These tools help us release and let go of our emotional baggage.

You may unconsciously be doing some of this work within yourself now, but it must become conscious to fully manifest. You must choose to realize the soul and spirit essence that you are.

Some people may seek psychological help when deciding to heal their emotional scars; good counseling always helps.

Other people simply take life one day at a time, working through their pasts by experiencing interactions with the people they are in contact with daily. In this manner, and without adequate tools for release, they tend to draw the same experiences to themselves continually. They question why the same things keep happening.

Although others may come and go in our life, the experiences they bring us do not. Until we are able to process and understand the meaning of our experiences, we will not be able to change them.

Without the help and tools we need for inner healing, we become weary of trying to figure out our problems. As we attempt to resolve our issues logically, we often feel that we are a victim of some cruel joke that God is playing on us. We feel that life is victimizing us and we question why all cannot simply be changed through logic and reason. Nevertheless, life rarely makes sense and the logical mind is little more than a storage center. All the rational mind has ever learned, all it contains, has been programmed through our life's learning experiences. The rational mind abilities are limited to the playback of learned images and responses, it does not have the capacity to feel or change itself. This can only be done by implementing new experiences and information.

We can learn to understand why we behave and react to situations the way we do, by observing our actions and ourselves. Doing this we identify past mental training and begin consciously changing our logical tapes. We can neither run away nor hide from our life experiences. Results come only through healing and integrating them.

MORALITY AND RELIGION

We often hear the statement "The moral fiber of this country", yet we have no way of knowing by whose standard this is determined. Morality is based on virtues and vices, the awareness of right and wrong.

I was raised a Catholic and went to church seven days a week. I was baptized, received communion and confirmed into the faith. I went to Catholic school and tried to be the best Catholic child that I could be.

Catholicism taught me as a child that I was a sinner in God's eyes, had always been a sinner, and would always be a sinner. Such beliefs taught me that I would never be good enough to gain God's approval.

Alternately at home, I was brought up believing that my parents felt the same way about me as God did. This constantly reinforced the belief within me, that I was not good enough. This moral training made me feel unworthy and ashamed of myself. I became isolated inside and wanted to hide what I came to believe was my ugliness.

Many of the world's societies believe that self-punishment and debasement lead to good moral living. Some religions, by instilling the belief that our very thoughts and desires make us sinners, teach us to suppress our emotions. This magnifies our sense of guilt and shame, which produces a tremendous emotional imbalance.

Since it is true that thought and desire create; these creations can only be changed by us understanding them, not by suppressing them. When we deny who we are emotionally, we stuff our feelings deep inside where they begin to fester. The result of this repression can and does manifest itself in many forms. Sometimes it manifests as mental illness, emotional instability, and various forms of physical pain and disease. Whole societies of people have and do become confused and hostile as the result of repressed emotions.

In true spiritual awareness, balanced emotions are the key to higher enlightenment. It is through our emotional experiences, that we gain the understanding necessary to control them. Our emotions are the only tool we have for learning how to love one another and our self.

Morality and spirituality are really the same thing. When we have moral values, we are naturally spiritual. Moral values should be taught and lived at home, not at church. The home should be the spiritual temple, and we should be worshipping spiritual values in life consistently. If we were to live life in this manner, true wisdom and insight would reveal itself and we would become *godlike*.

Most Western religions have become big business. No longer seeking to know and understand God, they choose to wield the power of God to fit their own mandates. Many religions use their teachings to brainwash and control people rather than helping them open up to god. This form of brainwashing convinces us that we should all think alike. Organizations such as these use this group energy to indoctrinate others into their sect.

Many of these religious organizations, herald themselves as Christians, becoming religious zealots who judge other faiths and label them as cults, not realizing they themselves have become just that.

More wars are fought in the name of religion than for any other reason. More people have died and been killed in the name of an all loving God than for any other cause. China executed the Tibetans, Serbia the Albanians; in Ireland, the Protestants and Catholics continue to fight; in Israel, it is the Muslims and Jews, all the way back to the Pagan Romans who persecuted the Christians. We have been through the Dark Ages, The Crusades, and The Spanish Inquisition.

Spiritual beliefs have always been a source of chaos on our planet and religious wars continue to ravage humanity. Some radical religionists condone bombing of abortion clinics and harassment of abortion doctors; they infiltrate public schools and politics, all in the name of Christ. War is waged on homosexuals, for some, this too is an abomination of God.

Many advocate the death penalty as justice for a crime, not seeing this as bias when they call abortion murder.

Taking of all or any human life is against God's law.

Somehow, somewhere in society, we have come to believe that if a person dies, he or she will not return. We need look to history to discover that problems do not go away by people killing one another. In fact, if all the people who have been killed never actually returned, why are there so many angry and distorted people on the planet now?

It seems that many religions conveniently make up God's rules as they go along. In this way, these organizations profess to know what God thinks. Their own teachings tell them that God is beyond their comprehension, yet inevitably they let their ego self¾their lower chakras—dictate truth.

The truth is vaster than any one being or book. The search for spiritual truth is the journey that brings eternal joy. The truth is an ever-expanding perception that is unending. Each person is a piece of this truth. When the pieces fit together, they make a beautiful picture that expands and changes as we all grow and develop. Some religions try to make this a still life picture rather than the ever-changing energy of life that it is.

When approaching religion, we should look at the life experiences brought about by the living examples of its believers in order to determine its values. If you find people who have opened their hearts and minds to become godlike by following the dictate of their religion, then there may be substance to their faith. If on the other hand, you find people of bigotry and judgment, or whose spirituality is lived only while in church, then be aware.

Remember that spirituality is not a religion. God has no religion, as God is pure spirit. Spirituality is the essence and energy that makes us all gods. If a religion does not teach its followers to live by this concept, it is not teaching spirituality.

Meditation

In your search for understanding, meditation is the stage where you begin to move from the outer realms of consciousness to the inner realms. Remember everything you are searching for lies hidden inside you. By accepting this truth, you become the greatest mystery available for your progression and exploration. Reaching this step allows you to shift from the visible to the invisible, the tangible to the intangible and from a solid state to fluid. Here motion becomes energy and flow, rather than mass and matter.

When working to truly understand the universe that we are, our perceptions begin change. We expand our thinking to include the awareness of how everything is really energy before it is anything else. Here we discover how energy itself is the creative principle in all life and how we ourselves are that ever moving, always-changing, self- same energy.

It is to meditation that we look to experience this understanding and awareness of being our true self. While in a meditative state one can learn to detach and observe the workings of their rational mind. This reasoning part of the brain is often the greatest deterrent to finding the inner self. In meditation we transition to find that space within ourselves that allows us to observe our own thoughts. In this manner, we discover the difference between who we think we are and who we truly are.

When you can sit in the quiet and observe how you think and feel, you are within consciousness. Now able to observe yourself, you begin ignoring the minds idle chatter. This allows you to move beyond your rationale and into the deeper dimensions of your being. In this altered state of consciousness, one feels and senses what is occurring rather than thinking about it. Experiencing yourself in this manner allows you to connect easily with your inner awareness and understanding.

It is quite common when returning from a meditative state, to a physical state of consciousness, to be unable to recall ones experiences. Even upon remembering, finding the proper words to describe what took place may be difficult. The meditative experience awakens us to the inner dimensions of the self that we long ago forgot. It may at first take time to consciously remember and decipher these journeys, be patient.

Exploring the inner dimensions of the self is always an exciting adventure. Quite often, beginning experiences are filled with colors and light. The colors experienced contain fascinating prisms and refractors, much like a light show at a planetarium. When we open our feeling senses and bask in the glow of multitudinous color we are enveloped by their essence. Try not to control this experience for doing so will end it. The meditative experience simply requires allowing and feeling. This is an exercise in trust.

The human body is reactionary and steeped in the instinct to survive. It automatically produces a sense of fear when entering the unfamiliar. In meditation, we are able move beyond this guardedness and into a sense of trust and allowing. This takes time and practice. Anything worth attaining is worth working at. Do not become discouraged or give up, keep trying.

Beginning meditation is like meeting a new friend. When it enters your life, you need to make a time and a place to spend with it. You must welcome meditation with an open heart and open arms. By doing so, you will find that meditation is the best friend you have ever had.

Meditative trance is unexplainable because there are no physical experiences with which to compare it. Experiencing the different meditative states of awareness becomes awesome. The more you practice the more proficient you become.

Beginning meditators, often describe similar experiences. The most frequently described are visions of geometric design and awe inspiring colors of light. This is the third eye or brow chakra beginning to open. This new way of seeing, through the feeling-self, allows us to experience movement of energy.

In a meditative state, one experiences a sense of no time and also a feeling of having gone somewhere. A feeling of warmth and lightness occur and we often feel aglow. Our everyday problems are put into new and different perspectives as our whole self, our whole being now perceives for us. A sense of peace pervades our very core and we feel connected with all other life. We can finally get above it all and relax our bodies and our minds.

Creating the time necessary to practice meditative disciplines seems to be reported by many as more difficult than the act itself. To achieve results, it is best in the beginning to sit and practice meditating at least three to five times a week for fifteen to twenty minutes each sitting. Once you set the time aside you can use it to listen to some calm meditative music if you choose. Here you can practice by letting the music envelop and carry you along. You can also take this time to create a sacred space for yourself while experiencing the energy of the light around you. Candles and incense, along with the music, can create a certain ambiance that will aid you in relaxing and meditating.

Reaching and attaining a God state of consciousness is the ultimate goal of meditation. Once we restore ourselves to our God consciousness, we realize how we are interconnected with all life; how all life is actually one thing, and how we are all one with that life. This awareness being activated, our life in the third dimensional world begins to change.

Once realizing that consciousness has always and will always exist, we can explore alternative ways of perceiving and living life. This new experience of ourselves as consciousness puts us in communion with our spirit essence. It is through our spirit self that we tap our inner wisdom and understanding and acceptance of our true destiny.

Through the development of this new communion, our spiritual nature will also help us to see the truth and reality of those others we care about in life. With this newfound clarity, we begin to see a different picture of life, a much grander picture that allows life to become a wondrous and exciting journey to behold and explore.

INITIATION

    We are all part of the natural order within life. The universe is ordered, nature is ordered and the divine is ordered.

    When we are in union with our divine essence we easily understand the divine order of life. Armed with this awareness, we can use the operation of divine order for the well being of the planet as well as for our selves. This we accomplish by observing the natural order of the life around us and by how we interact with it.

    When we go outdoors and away from the city, we discover a whole order of nature that works together in harmony. Each river and stream, each tree, plant and stone, seem to be strategically placed to work in harmony with one another. All of the animals serve a purpose through their nature as do insects, wind, fire, and rain. All these things work together to preserve the natural order of our planet. Humans are the only species upon the planet that do not naturally harmonize.

    Through a process of discovery, we learn that growth and development take time. We discover we must learn how to walk before we can run. We must learn our letters and numbers before we can put them together to read and write, add and subtract. We discover that a tree or flower must be seeded before it can grow. Ideally and necessarily, a parent teaches a child to survive and fend for itself before he or she goes out into the world. We are continually learning that there are elements in life to be overcome. These experiential lessons are our tests of inner strength that affect us both physically and spiritually. This is the order of life to which we adhere daily, living on this planet.

Opening to our divine nature is simply a beginning in our spiritual process of learning. We think that in realizing our divinity, we will be able to stop or change our soul karma; we deeply desire a magical experience that can change destiny. Getting in touch with our divine nature does not save us from ourselves, but puts us into the awareness of our true work. Within our divine nature lie the necessary tools for the understanding and patience needed to discover ourselves as a spirit being.

To change our destiny, we become the masters of it.

Human nature always seems to get in the way of us developing and using our spiritual tools accurately. Our rational and emotional conditioning continuously try to regiment our lives and destinies. Our human nature inclines us to be dissatisfied with ourselves and leads us to believe that by being someone other than ourselves will solve our problems. This makes it difficult for us to accept ourselves as who we are in the moment.

All things simultaneously exist in the present moment. We are able to experience all things at all times in a proper state of meditation. This is called multidimensional awareness. It is within this pure experiential state that we no longer think, but simply experience. In this experiential state, we learn entirely through a process of osmosis; here we are able to absorb the information needed to understand the dimensions of life. Spiritual enlightenment is achieved by using patience and allowing. When we learn to be detached and objective about ourselves, we learn to allow, in this way the answers we want and need easily come to us.

Our maturity spurts in life often appear as tests or initiations to us. These growth spurts occur in our spiritual development just as they do in our physical development. In order for us to remain integrated when our consciousness expands, all aspects of self must grow as well. All aspects of self are rooted within our chakra system. Each chakra emits a frequency and vibration known as a dimensional body; each of these bodies is consciousness and serves a specific role in our life.

The subtle body emitted from the root chakra is called the etheric body. The sacral chakra emits our emotional body; the solar plexus, the lower mental; the heart chakra, the astral body; the throat chakra, the causal body; the third eye chakra, the celestial body; and the crown emits the ketheric body or divine mind.

When our consciousness expands, all of the subtle bodies in our auric field are affected. It is when the soul memory within these bodies becomes activated that they realize their hunger for the spiritual food being offered them.

This is very similar to the changes we went through with the physical body when growing up. As our physical body grew larger, so did its capacity for food. Our taste buds changed as did our thinking and behaviors. It is the same with our newfound spiritual consciousness. The only difference is that now changes occur within all dimensions of self rather than just the physical.

Consciousness expansion may be likened to a volcanic eruption. Everything inside of you has to make way for whatever was trapped at the bottom. Sometimes when experiencing this great eruption we find that our life also erupts. To reiterate it is very much like growing up. When the physical body spurts, we get larger clothes and shoes. The bedroom becomes too small and we require more space. We even outgrow our parents' environment and learn to define our own. It is the same with spiritual growth.

As we grow spiritually, we often find out tastes in life begin to change. We outgrow the need for various people and places in life. We require more serenity and space for quiet contemplation.

Often we encounter resistance from those around us who do not understand or relate to the changes that we are experiencing. This feels like a test of strength.

Initiation is likened to a test when it is simply an expansion of self. This expansion is how we bring about the desired changes within our self as well as our life.

When energy expands in one place, it displaces energy in another. The displaced energy can only compensate by reorienting itself to become comfortable with the change. When an expansion of energy is continual, energy is unable to settle into a new comfort zone. When this happens we feel displaced. This means that we have already become too settled in a given comfort zone and do not know how to react when outside of it. Feeling unsettled and uncomfortable pushes us to grow and develop. Comfort zones are important but can hinder our progression when we become too attached to them.

True security can only be attained within. When we follow the inner journey toward our divinity, we realize that whatever we previously believed to be important probably was not. Many of the ideals not previously embraced, now become paramount as we break free from old concepts and ideas that locked us in an "ivory tower" of assumed security and comfort. Suddenly we want to break free of the passive thinking and actions that imprisoned our true character and potential. Breaking free becomes the goal and the challenge. This is initiation.

With initiation now in stride, we challenge our beliefs on every level. Our subtle bodies have been asleep–numb–for a very long time. As we hurl ourselves forward into expansion, our habits and beliefs pull strongly to hold us in place. Like a frightened child, we cling to the fear of change, often finding ourselves tired and dismayed, wanting only to break free of the struggle.

Our struggle comes from those aspects of ourselves that are afraid to learn and grow. Aspects of us that have never been taught, nor given the opportunity, to understand there was something beyond the complacent acceptance of what we thought life should be. These frightened aspects of self are terrified of the unknown path we now wish to explore, and so resist. Thus, now is the time to be still and go within.

It is within the stillness that we commune with these aspects of self and appease their fears.

As spiritual beings, we can teach our frightened aspects to overcome and trust in the new progression. We need to be patient with this process as it is important for these aspects to believe they are heard, loved and wanted so they can feel safe and heal. They may have felt alienated or inadequate for much of life and now need to find a place of understanding within you. Healing takes time. By giving yourself permission to go through the process, you will make the time to overcome any difficulty involved.

To achieve a state of blissful happiness, all the vibrational bodies in your energy field must be activated and developed. Until now, you have merely existed. Now you strive to be alive—REALLY ALIVE! You strive for interconnectedness and the spiritual nourishment that sustains all life.

Self-realization

    Spiritual understanding can only happen when inner divine truth is realized. At times, opening to our inner truth may seem painful, but it does free us to become fulfilled. With the understanding of spiritual truth in our life, our perceptions expand allowing us to see ourselves as the universe that we are.

    In order to achieve spiritual understanding we must examine ourselves thoroughly to discover how we are the reflection of life. With this accomplished, we no longer allow the outer world to determine our fate and our destiny. It is in this way of inner truth, that we discover and understand our divine nature.

    Self-realization in essence is divine in nature. True understanding of ones divinity can only be understood through self-awareness. One can achieve inner self-realization by experiencing the truth and light that dwell within.

    Once in the perception of spiritual understanding, we are free to conceptualize rather than rationalize. Conceptualization allows us to realize that what we believed reality to be, is merely one aspect of truth. Spiritual understanding is our key to awareness and truth. Like the strands of a tapestry, beautifully woven together, spiritual understanding, awareness, and truth are synonymous. Their weave, color, and beauty bring us a much greater perspective of life. A picture, if you will, filled with beauty, movement, resonance and love of life.

We can only understand how reality is multidimensional through the experience of being multidimensional. This we do through our process of realization. If we choose to live in a limited awareness that is constricted and shallow, we experience realizations about ourselves that are limiting. When our multidimensional growth is stifled, little if any true love or joy can be experienced. When we dwell in such a restrictive state, as hard as we try to discover the means for true happiness, we fall short. With human nature being insatiable, all joyous events become short lived.

When dwelling within spiritual wisdom we attain long-standing satisfaction with our self and life that is sustained eternally. Here within the spiritual self, we discover how to manifest our desires in a sustainable way.

It is through the realization of our three lower chakras that we have learned to survive.

Feeding ourselves, learning to walk and realizing we could read or write are all lower chakra accomplishments needed for physical survival. Through survival, we have developed the ability to think for ourselves, to overcome crises, and tackle new challenges. These things we accomplished by realizing how to do them. Without the acceptance that we can accomplish a specific task, we will never realize our ability to do so.

Now that we have realized we can survive physically, it is time to realize how to survive spiritually. Just as the body and mind require nourishment, so does the soul and spirit. If any aspect of our self is deprived nourishment, the other aspects also suffer malnutrition. If we do not feed the body, it will die. If we do not feed the mind, it will be ignorant. If we do not feed the soul, it stagnates.

The soul requires acknowledgment and care, just as the mind and body does. By opening to the realization of this fact we connect with our soul's energy and begin to acknowledge its purpose in our life. This is how we begin to feed the soul.

Recognizing your soul as the energy that transports you from incarnation to incarnation is primary. This recognition ignites the interaction between you and your soul-self. Acknowledging the soul, re-opens us to the inner awareness that soul contains all of the memory of who we are, have been, and will be. Soul was designed to be this vehicle. This acknowledgment allows direct communion with the soul self. This is the beginning of self-realization.

We cannot accomplish self-realization if we deny the true essence of ourselves as eternal beings. It is only through communion with the eternal Self that we can become self-realized.

In seeing ourselves as eternal rather than temporal, we begin to understand the true scope of what life is. It is within this spiritual understanding that we experience the sacredness of life and realize the flow of energy to which all life belongs.

Denial of the eternal Self has been accepted as a norm for many centuries. When humans lose their connection to their eternal awareness and understanding, they suffer continuously lifetime after lifetime, wondering why life is filled with desperation and destitution. They feel void of any true feelings of love and compassion and become severely depressed.

People who are aware of their souls, are calling to the energies of these lost souls and constantly asking them to return and help humans remember their eternal selves. Helping people acknowledge their eternal essence by becoming self-realized will help restore harmony to earth.

Self-realization is the process necessary for the continuation of true spiritual evolution. Without it, the species of humankind will not be fulfilled; our spiritual destiny will wither into destruction and devastation. Being the gods that we essentially are, every individual has choice, and each of us makes a difference as to the checks and balances of the whole. Through just one awareness, the balance can be swayed for the many. It is your turn now to choose the path of enlightenment.

Only through choice, commitment, and spiritual discipline can we attain true spiritual understanding and love. Self-realization is the key to successful, happy living. We must all learn to be free to create in harmony with the life that surrounds us. We must learn to restore balance where there is chaos and give love where this is none. Loving self is what we discover through realization. When we understand how we are love then we understand how all things are love. It is in this way that the balance shall be restored.

Enlightenment

Enlightenment is not a term or a word but an experience. When one is enlightened, they are aware of how they belong within the whole. They become aware that they are spirit within, and they live in an integrated state of higher awareness.

Becoming enlightened is the nature of the journey that was taken on when choosing to be born into the third dimension. Becoming spiritually enlightened is the fulfillment of this journey.

Once spiritually enlightened one begins to see and live the "bigger picture". This "bigger picture," allows us to comprehend the true purpose of existence. Without true purpose in life, we go through the motions of life, never understanding its rhyme or reason. This leads us to question forever our purpose in being here.

As we develop and become spiritually enlightened, we realize that there is an order to life. An order that goes far beyond anything we may have learned through our life experiences or academic learning. A divine order with pristine laws based in perception and understanding. These are natural laws, ordering the Universe and the Cosmos and all life beyond.

These laws have motion and movement. These laws have been given names such as "The law of Cause and Effect. The Law of Attraction, The law of Karma, The law of Rebirth,

The Law of Science and Mathematics (also known as Sacred Geometry) and others I cannot name.

These laws can only be learned and understood conceptually. To the rational being they make very little if any sense at all. It is the soul consciousness that remembers and uses these laws to live by.

In order to familiarize yourself with these theoretical laws you might explore books on Quantum Physics and Metaphysics. By doing so, perhaps you can use the left part of your brain as a relay to tap the subconscious and super-conscious.

There is no more rewarding or greater journey than that of spiritual enlightenment. Enlightenment is the one thing we can accrue this lifetime that we can not only take with us, but can also use as our vehicle to explore the heavenly worlds of evolution when we die.

When we leave this earthly body, many humans believe that we automatically ascend to these heavenly worlds. Realize simply, that one must know God here, before one can know god anywhere else.

We dwell continually within many worlds while alive in the physical, whether we are aware of it or not. Little is different after we cross over. Unawareness carries over to the other side just as awareness does. Our realizations while in the physical, have much, if not all, to do with what our realities will be when we cross over. Life after death is not a reprieve from our life on earth; rather an extension of the journey already created.

Without spiritual enlightenment here, there can be no spiritual enlightenment elsewhere for us. There is no magic wand that God waves when you die to save you from your own dysfunctional perceptions. Truly the realizations that you experience on the other side, can only be used when you are re-incarnated to try to get it right the next time.

If instead we were to take responsibility for our own spiritual enlightenment this lifetime, beginning to realize how we and God are one and the same, imagine the changes we could produce in our own evolutionary paths. Many less dysfunctional beings would be returning to the earth plane each round and a more spiritually advanced culture could begin designing and healing the future of humanity.

"The only things in Life that will ever let you down are your expectations."

—Archangel Raphael

PART II - WORKBOOK

"Find your sword of truth and Live it.
Make your life the reality you want."

—Archangel Michael

THE WORKBOOK

Everything in part two of this book will help you assist yourself in the process of spiritual development. The exercises I share here are exercises I myself use and also teach in my classes. You may feel a bit odd or silly when first practicing these, but after a time, you will find they become a great comfort.

You are entering on a new journey, a new school of learning. Begin with an open mind and heart, without judgment or criticism. Enter your new learning space as if in kindergarten with all the newness and enthusiasm you can imagine. Overcome your apprehension and fear by allowing yourself to anticipate the outcome as one of joy and fulfillment.

Keep a journal of your progress as you go and make a commitment to follow through. You can attain profound results in just six months to a year's time. Remember to be patient. Anything worth having is worth the time and energy spent.

Creating a sacred space is a very important element of protecting yourself when working on yourself. Just as we automatically put on our seat belt in the car, we want to be in the light of the divine as we do our spiritual work. When we create sacred space, we acknowledge our connection with the divine thereby aligning its energy to assist us. We are at the same time using our divine energy to anchor Light and Love on the planet, assisting the universe in helping all those that we love.

May you always be in light.

CREATING A SACRED SPACE

To begin setting the energies for your meditation and inner healing work you need to place yourself in a space of resonation with the divine. It is for this reason that you cleanse and purify the space you are using to receive divine help and guidance. You may wish to purchase and use a variety of tools to enhance the sacred energies in your space. These can aide in the conductivity of the sacred energies you are invoking.

Some useful tools:
- Candles
- Sea Salt
- Incense
- Crystals
- Scented Oils
- Prayers and Invocations
- Small altar

To begin creating your sacred circle of light you take some sea salt water and sprinkle it clockwise around you in a circle saying:

"I do hereby purify this space, with the waters of earth and with salt, so that I may connect within the purity of my divine light."

Following the water purification you take your incense and retrace your circle saying:

"By the power of fire and air I protect and seal my sacred space, that it may be innocent and pure."

You are now ready to honor the Four Universal Directions of North, East, South and West.

North corresponds to the element of Earth.
East corresponds to the element of Air.
South corresponds to the element Fire.
West corresponds to the element of Water.

All life as we know it is made up of these four elements. We put ourselves in harmony with the energies, of Earth, Air, Fire and Water, by invoking and acknowledging them.

We physically are made up of these four elements ourselves. Our bodies are two-thirds water, our mind is air or thought, our spirit is fire and the warmth of our body is made of the same nutrients as earth herself.

Now face the direction of North and state:

"I invoke the energies of Mother Earth and her great protectors. I invoke her love. I thank her for the food she produces, the dwelling I live in and the clothes on my back. Mother Earth I honor you."

Close your eyes and let yourself connect with the energy you feel in this direction.

Now do a chant, an AUM, or ring a chime.

Now turn and face the direction of the East and state:

"I invoke the energies of the guardians of Air and of the element of Air itself. I ask for the alignment and attunement of my inner understanding of my spiritual mind. Mighty element of air, open within me now and guide my thoughts and prayers."

Close your eyes and let yourself connect with the energy you feel from this direction.

Now do a chant or AUM, or ring a chime.

Now turn and face the direction of the South and state:

"Mighty spiritual light of fire. Power of the Sun. I invoke and call to you now. Bring your warm sunlight into my heart and soul. Make me whole. Great element of fire I honor you."

Close your eyes and let yourself connect with the energy you feel from this direction. Now say a chant, or AUM or ring a chime.

Now turn to the west and state:

"Mighty waters of the earth I honor and call to you. Inner emotions all align and open to truth. May the tides of man be calm and may peace prevail. I attune now to the motion of universal Light."

Close your eyes and let yourself connect with the energy you feel from this direction. Now do a chant, an AUM or ring a chime.

You may now choose to light one or more candles in your sacred space. Surrounding yourself with crystals may feel comforting or even burning a candle at each of the four directions. You will intuit what feels appropriate as you progress and practice.

Now that the space has been set you may wish to meditate, say prayers and invocations, or just listen to some soothing music that allows you to feel peaceful. Sacred space can be used to say prayers, to communicate with divine teachers and guides of love or even to do visualizations. It is your sacred space, use it for whatever pleases you in the moment. Be spontaneous.

Creating a sacred space helps understand how the divine and we are one. The divine is never in a hurry and always is at peace. By creating this energy yourself, you learn what it means to resonate. Energy is all resonation. You are always a resonation within the divine energy of all life. Play within this energy and learn to honor your divine self.

Sacred Space Stress Exercise

Sit or lie, breathing deeply for five breaths. As you focus on your breathing, begin counting your heartbeats. Feel your body letting go of all the stress and concerns it's been holding.

Imagine yourself floating on the water with ease allowing the water to simply hold you up. Feel the warmth of the sun as it radiates down upon you. See the brightness of its rays. Hear the water lapping beneath you and sense the air as it touches your face. Remain here in this wonderfully relaxed state recharging your batteries

Do this stress exercise before going to sleep or use to take you into meditation.

INVOCATIONS AND PRAYERS

Invocations and prayers can be used to center your energies. They are powerful alone or as a lead into your meditation. Using invocations and prayers should become a new habit that helps relieve tension and invokes the aide of the higher powers of light into your sphere.

Here are some examples you may wish to use.

I call forth the power of light that I am. I call forth my higher self, my guides, my teachers and all who assist me in my greater understanding of the light within that I am. I ask that these energies of light align within me to aid in the process of self-understanding. By the power of light within that I Am, I decree this be so in the name of the Father, the Mother, The Son and The Holy Spirit, Amen.

Heavenly Father, Divine Mother, I call you forth and ask that you anchor your light in and around me, so that what is needed for my highest and best purpose be mine today. I honor the Father and Mother energy of all life and align myself to the balance of male female within. May your blessings be powerful and kind. May you assist all humanity. I am that I am... I am that I am.... I am that I am.

(The" I Am", is the resonation of yourself within God.)

I call to the Mighty Archangels of Light. Lord Raphael, Lord Michael, Lord Gabriel and Lord Ariel. Most holy angels and teachers of light hear my call. Know that I am a humble servant of god who serves the cause of humankind. Help me to remember and re-align to my soul purpose and destiny this lifetime. Open my awareness to rekindle the eternal flame that burns within. Show me the way to become a knowing participant in the wondrous events taking place on the earth at this time.

I am, I am, I am a beautiful child of light,
I am, I am, I am, the most Holy Spirit of light.
I am, I am, I am eternal in my light.
I ask now for my eternal divine essence to make itself known to me today and always.
Beloved I am, Beloved I am, Beloved I am.

Invocation to the Holy Light Within

I CALL FORTH THE POWER OF LIGHT THAT I AM

I AM THAT I AM
I AM THAT I AM
I AM THAT I AM

I AM EARTH
I AM AIR
I AM FIRE
AND I AM WATER

I CALL TO MY TEACHERS AND MY GUIDES
I CALL TO MY HIGHER SELF, MY SPIRIT ESSENCE AND MY HOLY LIGHT
I CALL TO THE RADIANT LIGHT OF SOURCE

IMBUE ME WITH THE LIGHT AND WISDOM NECESSARY TO SURRENDER TO MY SPIRITUAL LIGHT. KNOW THAT I AM A CHILD OF LIFE WHO SERVES THE CAUSE OF SPIRIT IN ALL. BRING YOUR ENERGY, BRING YOUR LIGHT I IMPLORE THEE.

BELOVED I AM, BELOVED I AM, BELOVED I AM.

What is processing?

We process to help us to let go of old emotional, physical and mental baggage. Using process techniques, we can learn to change existing patterns and implement others. We are actually in some form of unconscious process all of the time. Using specialized exercises we consciously attune to this work and achieve a much greater degree of healing and integration.

We promote the healing of ourselves emotionally, mentally and spiritually by the use of our new processing tools. Presently we are little more than the accepted programs created from our pasts. By recognizing this fact, we shall change and create a new life for our self, a life that includes mind, body, soul and spirit.

It is time for all of us to become our own therapists. We need to take responsibility for the inner healing that needs to take place so we can manifest the desired result into our outside world.

The following are exercises that are used as a process of healing through the chakras and the subtle bodies. Our chakras and subtle bodies are what make up the Aura that surrounds us. This aura is our life giving force. It is seen through clairvoyance as an emanation of light surrounding the physical body. This auric field of light and energy should be cleansed and aligned regularly for it to harmonize itself to its highest and best purpose, both physically and spiritually.

With the proper diligence and applied stamina, you will obtain deserved success and rewards.

Here is an example of how processing works:

You are seeking to become gainfully employed. You have plenty of qualifications, yet it seems that none of the doors are opening for you. You immediately feel as if you are being punished. You mentally beat yourself up and become depressed. You feel as if the world is out to get you.

In this circumstance, you are blocked by feelings of depression, self-abuse, and the need to be punished. These feelings—conditions—exist within you as an accepted way of being. They probably come up in life every time you are forced to change. This past conditioning is what needs to be integrated and healed in order for you to feel free to move forward in life. You begin by identifying each of these feelings individually and working through them.

Where in your life did this feeling originate? What were the circumstances? How old were you when you can first remember feeling this way? Who was involved?

All of these questions help you begin to dig into the buried recess of the past. Here is where the conditioning started and here is where you must heal it.

These first steps of contemplation can be very helpful. By simply taking a little quiet time and allowing yourself to identify your feelings and when they started, helps you to see just how long the have been that way. Remembering others that were involved, helps you see where forgiveness is needed. Remembering certain circumstances shows you how you have re-created the circumstance over and over again.

Another example:

You are on your third marriage or live-in relationship. When you met this person, you were sure that the relationship would last forever. This was finally the perfect match.

This relationship begins triggering old emotional responses inside. Suddenly you doubt your own feelings. Feelings of "having made a big mistake" begin to surface causing you anxiety and fear. You experience the same patterns coming to life in this relationship as in your previous relationships. You start believing that this new mate no longer seems to be the person you thought he or she was. You no longer feel that sense of trust and safety.

This circumstance presents you with patterning that is deeply imbedded within you. The culprit here is past experiences of betrayal. It is your issue and you must own it (admit it) to yourself.

You have always believed, it was the other person who needed to change. It is time to address the issue as being your own so you can take responsibility for your choices and your feelings. Now you can begin to process the patterns and conditions inside that continually draw you to this type of relationship. Experience has taught us that we cannot change another; that is something only they can do. We can facilitate a change only by first changing us.

Our conditioning from the past can only be changed when we acknowledge the problem or situation for what it is. We must take responsibility for our own feelings, admitting another cannot heal them. If we feel the feeling, it is ours no matter who else might be involved. This is a hard concept to grasp. Our learning in life has been to blame someone or something else for the way we feel and perceive. By doing so, we eliminate the need to grow beyond this way of being.

This is how we stay stuck in the past.

Our conditioning:

Now let us look at the conditioning brought about by typical life experience.

In school, you learned the ABCs, addition and subtraction, history and geography, as well as, to read, write and perform properly in the presence of adults. All this academic training and etiquette, is carried through, and defines who you are in your daily life. We appreciate the learning and training we received in these areas. These experiences taught us how to live in society and care for ourselves financially.

All past experiences are stored somewhere in our memory. Our memory continually plays back the information we have previously stored and we use that information to experience ourselves every day. Our feelings experience things in this same manner.

The feelings you experienced as a child, adolescent, teenager and adult, have become accepted patterns within you. You use them to identify yourself. These patterns are your make-up–the so-called "normal" you. These accepted patterns are the person you know yourself to be, your identity, your persona.

The inner-self has to do with feelings and concepts, imagination and creativity. We tend to get caught, in our personality self, and forget to develop the inner-self.

We are unconscious of the learning process within the feeling self as it happens very subtly.

Just as academic information is stored in the mind, so feeling information becomes stored in the body. This is why changing your mind cannot, by itself, change how you feel.

All the learning you stored up to this point can only be used by remembering it. Confused? If this concept is confusing to you, it is because the mind's program is to believe it controls us. Yet we need only to examine the various diseases and an illness throughout society, to see how little control the mind actually has over the body.

Example:

Take for example someone being diagnosed with a terminal illness. The first reaction to such news is disbelief. In the individual's mind, it surely cannot be so. Even though the mind cannot change the fact that the disease exists in the body, it refuses to acknowledge the truth. Here the emotions take over.

Once this person has processed the shocking news, he or she battles with himself or herself to come to terms with it. The resignation to the news as being accurate allows them to accept the disease as a fact. Both the feeling self and the rational mind reach this understanding together. Though the feeling self acknowledges the truth, the mind may continue to battle in disbelief or vice a versa.

If this individual chooses not to accept this disease as the end of their life, then the whole person begins the fight to live a disease-free and healthy life. The rational mind alone does not make this choice. It is both the mind and feeling self.

We will now examine criminal offenders as an example of an existing condition in society. Many people believe that these individuals have no desire to change. Yet if we are always seeking to achieve a better and happier future for ourselves why do we believe that they do not want the same? Just because someone has lived horrible experiences, does not mean he or she likes it that way or would not change it if they could.

Within all human beings is an innate desire,

To do well and to have a better life.

Perhaps the conditions surrounding such people did not teach them a way in which to create patterning that would allow them to do good things. If the opportunity were present, along with a means of accomplishing the end, these individuals might jump at it.

Criminals are a symptom of what has gone wrong in the world. Just as the body shows symptoms of an illness, so crime shows us symptoms of an ill society. So much terrorism and criminal activity is like a cancer, eating our world alive. This negativity grows and feeds off itself.

People have become de-sensitized by the world and environment in which they dwell. The negativity we call crime, is an *out of balance state*, of the feeling self. When people do not feel good about themselves, they cannot feel good about anything. This causes them to become diseased and ill. These illnesses are emotional as well as physical.

The Pattern of Abuse:

Studies in the USA tell us that most people who abuse have themselves been abused. Now rationally, if you had suffered abuse in your life, would you knowingly wish to inflict it on anyone else? People who inflict abuse cannot find a rational reason for doing so. They act out of an unconscious need to express their own pain and suffering; they rarely consciously choose to hurt others.

This shows us how powerfully imbedded conditioning and patterning can be. Changing patterns of abuse take great effort and determination. When individuals, have been physically, verbally or even sexually abused, the damage is buried deep inside. Many even completely block out the mind's memory of the attack; experiences such as these lead to de-sensitization.

The memory of such events festers like an open wound deep inside the feeling self. Most find themselves acting out in a dysfunctional manner and wondering why. The painful inner memories are like an infection that spreads through their life making them feel out of control or mentally unbalanced. They can develop phobias such as obsession and paranoia. They often try to self-medicate using drugs and alcohol. Ingrained patterning such as this leads to many forms of self and other abuse.

It is during the early formative years of life that our strongest patterning and conditioning takes place. It was during our growing up years that we were subjected to family and societal conditioning. We modeled ourselves to develop these patterns and this is who we know ourselves to be. It was in this way that we became a product of our environment.

As children we were like sponges absorbing all the emotions and thought patterns surrounding us. We received it all making it our own.

If our parents, family members, and/or caretakers were filled with unconditional love and acceptance, so probably are we. If they wholeheartedly accepted themselves and others for who they are, so shall we. Unfortunately being brought up in an environment such as this is unusual, if not unlikely. Even with a lot of unconditional love in the home the outside world still holds a great influence.

In life there is always a paradox. Without the depth of pain and sadness, we can never really understand the depth of true joy and happiness. The two of these together, pain and joy bring the awareness of harmony. No matter how much goodness we experience, we must also experience its opposite to truly understand and appreciate it.

Now consider the conditions in your own life. If you could change how you feel about yourself and the world, would you do it?

The two most elusive things in life are love and happiness and yet they are free. When we are missing these important elements in life, we tend to become morose and despondent. We find ourselves living a kind of robotic existence, never really knowing or caring to understand why we feel so detached and separate. We lose hope.

To change this, it becomes imperative to discover your true inner self, the natural you. That being that resides inside you who remembers what it is like to be unencumbered by conditioning. The being who wants to cleanse them self of the many robes they have worn this lifetime and open to a new way of creating and living life. You, "the inner being", choosing to remember its purity and love so as to live life in a renewed manner.

Tapping this inner self is how we get off the merry-go-round of life. Here we begin participating rather than going through the motions of living. We can now become the creators of our own reality, taking the time to fully savor it.

In modern society, so much of "life" takes place in the movies and on TV that we have become accustomed to observing rather than initiating. We see and experience so much drama in daily life that it has become accepted as real and normal. Many people have no awareness of living outside turmoil and chaos. Their existence has become so painful that they feel they must escape. Many of them turn to drugs, alcohol and violence, while others find solace in food or exercise. Some people become "couch potatoes" while others lose themselves in religion.

Trying to escape our soul experience by hiding or losing our self will not work; we cannot deny the existence of our soul by escaping a life we do not like nor understand. Just as we are physical beings, we need to acknowledge that we are soul beings and begin nurturing our soul and feeling self. In this way and this way alone, can we achieve living a healthy and fulfilling life.

Your body and feeling self, need to absorb life in a way, that allows them to express their feelings healthily. These aspects of self, want to be acknowledged, and experienced, just as the mind does. Through process exercise, you allow this expression to take place and become consciously aware of what is happening within you.

To truly be happy and a participant in life, we all need to mentally and emotionally process.

We always unconsciously "process" in some manner, but doing so unconsciously causes us confusion and the feeling of helplessness. Taking a personal and conscious initiative puts you in the position of mastering and changing your destiny.

The American Heritage Dictionary of the English Language defines *process* as "a series of actions, changes, or functions that bring about an end or result." You process to attain a desired result.

It is said, "Rome wasn't built in a day"; and neither were your *accepted* patterns and conditions created overnight. Be patient! It will take time to create the new you.

The uninhibited natural being has first to emerge for you to begin employing a change. Once initiated, this change process will gather momentum. Although you may not know exactly when or how the new changes take place, they simply will. We have all been designed to live happy and fulfilled lives. This innate desire dwells within each of us.

The Natural You

Much of what you will discover as you process your learned responses has to do with who you are *naturally*. The American Heritage Dictionary defines *natural* as "present in or produced by nature; not artificial or man-made. Pertaining to or produced solely by nature, or the expected order of things."

Our natural being is a pure unaltered state of who we are. As such humans, we are each quite an exceptional being with a great uniqueness and beauty. We also have a great deal of untapped creativity just waiting to be explored and used!

Sticking to and using process techniques can unclog the drain and get you running smoothly again. You all know what it feels like to be blocked and backed up. There comes a time in life when we all get tired of watching everyone else attain in life those goals we cannot seem to reach. It is time to stop watching life through the window and finally enter in through the door.

Processing is a major door for those who wish to use and develop with it. The natural you is waiting inside to be rediscovered. The natural you has perhaps been stuffed away and hidden but not discarded.

Process Exercises

1. Always begin by writing things down. A journal is most helpful to track your progress.

2. To begin, make a list of the things about yourself you want to change. These conditions may be ones of doubt, shame, guilt, self-abuse, fear, and so forth. These can be written like *"I choose to be guilt free", " I choose to change how I feel about my guilt", "I choose to release my thoughts and patterns of fear and limitation".*

    You may just choose to make a list such as, "I want to change feeling ashamed all the time." or "I want to change feeling out of control with my anger."

3. Write your commitment to change your conditioning. Commit to spending a select amount of time each week working on those changes. For example:
   *"I now make the commitment to myself to change _____.
   I now choose to set aside one hour every other day to work on this."*

4. Set a goal for a year's time to see desired results.

5. Write a daily journal about what is happening within you and in your life.

Getting to the Heart

6. Actively seek professional help, if you need it.

7. Set up a program of books to read, and classes/workshops that will be helpful.

8. You have now set your intent.

"You are the power and the light
that can change your life"

—Athene

What are Chakras

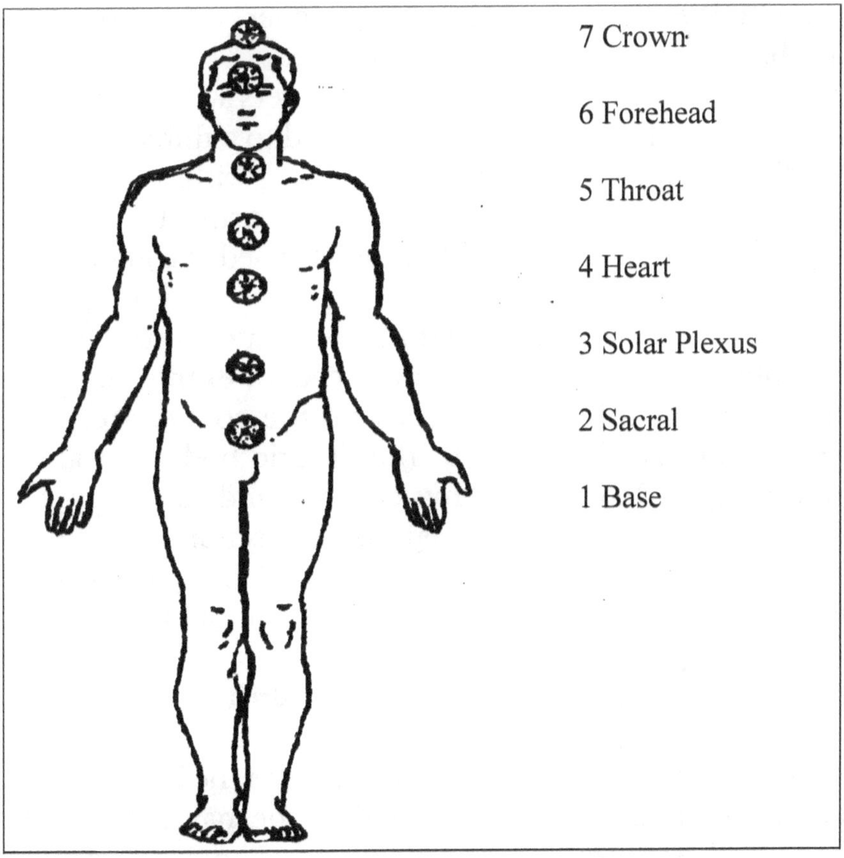

7 Crown

6 Forehead

5 Throat

4 Heart

3 Solar Plexus

2 Sacral

1 Base

The chakras are a valuable tool for learning to work within other dimensions. The ancient teachings of the chakra's can be studied and read about in philosophies and religions such as Buddhism, Brahman, Hinduism, and Theosophy. Books by many renowned healers and teachers on this subject are included at the end of the book.

The chakra system in the physical body makes up the auric field, or auric egg that surrounds us. The aura is made up of a group of electromagnetic fields of energy that are emitted from the chakras. This energy field surrounding the body is our life force. Some believe this energy to be our Chi. I believe that our chakra system energy is beyond Chi, but that Chi is contained within it.

There are seven main energy centers within the auric field. Each of these wheels is connected to a different plane, or dimensional awareness that exists within everyone. some of these fields of energy are more active than others; depending on the areas of life most stressed at a given time.

Chakra number 1 (see diagram) — located at the base of the spine or coccyx. When doing chakra exercises, to feel the energy of this chakra, focus on the coccyx area. This base chakra is connected to the etheric body and affects everything to do with the physical body and its energy. This chakra receives energy through its connection to the earth, and supplies the body with pure physical energy. The color associated with this chakra is red, the color of blood.

Called the Mooladhara Chakra in Sanskrit.

Chakra number 2 — the sacral center in the body, located along the spinal column, just below the navel. The color associated with this chakra is orange. The sacral center's body in the energy field is the emotional body. This is a very powerful and active center, because so much of what we do and understand is affected by our emotions. When we are stuck emotionally at a certain age or stage; our memories are stored within the emotional body and sacral chakra. The color associated with this chakra is vibrant orange.

In Sanskrit "Sadhisthana Chakra.

Chakra number 3 — the solar plexus chakra, located along the spinal column approximately one inch above the navel. The color associated with this chakra is yellow. Within the solar plexus, we experience anxiety and fear. Panic attacks, or being gripped by fear, affect all three lower chakras but usually manifest through the solar plexus. Many people who live a fear-based life often experience stomach problems because the solar plexus chakra shuts down due to an overload of fear and anxiety. This chakra relates to the mental body.

In Sanskrit "Mani Puri chakra"

Chakra number 4 — the heart chakra, located along the spinal column directly behind the heart. This chakra is connected to the astral body. The color associated with this chakra is emerald green.

The heart chakra and upper chakras are the spiritual centers. They are used less than the lower three, even though they help you balance and understand the true meaning of your life. This is because they are not needed in everyday physical survival. We can pick up a fork and eat without using them, we can earn a living or take ourselves down the street without using them, but we cannot experience a richness or fullness of life without their activation and development. Our upper three chakras allow us to commune with our soul self/God self and collective self.

The heart chakra itself is the bridge of consciousness that leads us to the awareness and understanding of our spirituality. Through activation and understanding of the heart chakra, we can transcend the painful experiences of our past. The heart chakra also is the key to balancing our dual spiritual and animal nature. This center brings about illumination of our human self.

Unconditional love resides in the heart chakra. The lower chakras contain conditional experiences and conditional love. Most people have closed their heart chakra due to the pain and priority of survival.

Ultimately, the fourth chakra—the heart—helps you to remember what it is like to be truly loved. The heart center pulls your lower centers into a close relationship with unconditional love, allowing you to explore that consciousness. This process aids you in discovering the higher purpose of each lower center. The chakra centers and the subtle energy bodies do not function separately, they work together to help us evolve and grow.

In Sanskrit "Anahata Chakra"

Chakra number 5 — the throat chakra, located just behind the throat along the spinal column. The color associated with this chakra is a beautiful sky blue. This chakra is connected to the "causal" body, which is the energy body of consciousness that dwells within the realm of "cause and effect". When you have activated and learned to utilize this subtle body, you are in contact with the natural laws that govern you. This availability allows us to change our life through manifestation.

In Sanskrit The " Vissudhi Chakra"

Chakra number 6 — the brow or third eye chakra, located slightly above and between your two physical eyes. The color associated with this chakra is indigo. The brow chakra is connected to your celestial energy body. This chakra is the center of clairvoyance. It opens inward; this occurs when the other centers are aligned and the subconscious and conscious parts of your brain are in balance. When your third-eye chakra is operational, you are able to vision within other dimensions. Often this is the first spiritual center to open. It assists us greatly with the heart.

In Sanskrit "The Ajna Chakra"

Chakra number 7 — the crown chakra, located in the body at the top of your head where your soft spot was. The colors associated with this chakra are gold and violet. This chakra is connected to the ketheric body. The crown chakra is the God-Self center and the center of pure divine enlightenment. This center is your connection to the spirit essence you are, and your super-conscious mind.

At every placement of these divine chakra centers, there also is a physical gland. The proper operation of this glandular infrastructure affects your physical well-being in every way. Tapping into the awareness available through our energy centers is necessary if we are to lead healthy and happy lives.

In Sanskrit "Sahasrara Chakra"

Centering Exercise to Align Your Chakras

This exercise helps you to align your chakras through the use of sound and color. The sound for this exercise will be your own voice. To receive the full impact, speak the following statements aloud on a regular basis. This centering meditation can be used alone or before any other exercises.

Set aside a certain amount of time for each day when you will be uninterrupted while you do your processing, unplug or turn off the telephone. Do the exercises in silence, or with soothing background music. Sit (or lie down). Take a few deep breaths.

Then repeat aloud the following statement:

I call forth my root chakra, the etheric body connected to it, and the light of life within.

Feel yourself being enveloped in a vibrant red orb or flame of light. Focus on the base of your spine where the root chakra is located. Sense and feel the energy of this chakra. Feel yourself becoming absorbed into the red color. Allow yourself to *be* with the experience for a few minutes.

Follow the above steps with each of the following chakras: State:

I call forth my sacral chakra, the emotional body connected to it, and the light of life within.

Feel the orb or flames of light turn a vibrant orange. Focus on the spinal column just below the navel.

Now State:

I call forth my solar plexus chakra, the mental body connected to it, and the light of life within.

Feel the orb or flame of light turn bright yellow, like the sun. Focus on the area just above the navel, between the ribs.

Now State:

I call forth my heart chakra, the astral body connected to it, and the light of life within.

Feel the orb or flame of light turn emerald green, all the beautiful green colors of mother earth. Focus on the area of your heart.

Now State:

I call forth my throat chakra, the causal body connected to it, and the light of life within.

Feel the orb or flames of light turn sky blue. Focus on your throat area.

Now State:

I call forth my brow chakra, the celestial body connected to it, and the light of life within.
Feel the orb or flame of light turn indigo. Focus on the center of your brow.

Now State:

I call forth my crown chakra, the ketheric body connected to it, and the light of life within.

Feel the orb or flame of light turn gold. Focus on the area at the top of your head. As you feel your crown chakra open, bring that wonderful color of gold down throughout your spinal column, cleansing and purifying with the golden light all your other chakras.

Now state:

"I align myself to the Divine Light of energy that I am. I open to my spirit self and honor the light within. I am a creation of divine love."

When practicing this exercise you may feel more of a connection to some colors than others. Allow yourself extra time to sit with each color that feels good to you. Experience yourself becoming the color.

Colors are fun and scintillating energies to work with. Trying different colors of light bulbs in a room or a color light may help you experience them better.

This exercise is continually useful for getting in touch with your energetic subtle bodies and aligning your chakras. By implementing this exercise daily, you begin noticing that you feel more peaceful and relaxed. You also may notice a change in the way you think and perceive.

Forgiveness

The past, present, and future each exist within one another. They are the makeup that creates our picture of life and ourselves. Our past cannot be put behind us by us not thinking about it. Our training has been that by stuffing our emotions we can put things out of our mind.

Stuffing ones emotions year after year causes one to feel alienated and distant. It is all right to put our feelings on the back burner for a little while, but too often, we forget to bring them back to the foreground. This can cause us to lose perspective of self and others around us.

How well we process and understand our feelings determines our emotional health. Due to the emotional distress most individuals have suffered in life, they believe themselves unable to trust their feeling self.

When we push the emotions deep into the recesses of our being we isolate and insulate, losing our ability to deal with the intimate emotional situations in our personal lives. This in turn causes us loss in our ability to use logic and reason to resolve emotional situations in our lives.

In order to achieve good health or peace of mind it is necessary for us to bring our emotions into balance with our reason. Denying how we feel about different situations in our lives can be very self-destructive. We think that by stuffing our emotions they will go away.

Unexpressed emotions simply lie beneath the surface smoldering, waiting for an opportunity to emerge. Repressed emotions will eventually find a way of showing themselves. They are often released unexpectedly in a fit of anger, along with crying or yelling for no apparent reason. They can create mood swings and suicidal or homicidal thoughts. Depression, anxiety, stress, uncontrollable laughter, and crying are all symptoms of pent up emotions. We label this as mental illness and doctors prescribe drugs and other treatments. Nevertheless, no matter what we call it, the fact remains it is repressed emotion.

Often repressed emotions also manifest themselves through physical illness. Heart disease, arthritis, obesity, cancer, diabetes, and many other illnesses are more connected to the emotions than we think. Sometimes the result of repressed emotions can be terminal.

Forgiveness is the most powerful tool we have for dealing with repressed emotions. We all feel victimized by the seeming injustices that take place in our lives. Few of us know how to react to or process these feelings.

By learning to forgive yourself, other people, and the circumstances that have occurred in life, your experience of life becomes transformed. This transformation takes place not by us paying lip service to forgiving but by seriously delving within ourselves to admit that we are the one who has been repressing our emotions. We must each make a conscious effort to do whatever it takes to make peace with ourselves and the past.

If you carry a feeling of hatred around inside of yourself for twenty years or so, it eats away at <u>you</u> daily; not those you believe you hate. By harboring an intense feeling of hatred, you begin to attract others into your life that are harboring the same feeling. Together, you now feed off each other's hatred and begin finding fault with one another. This happens because like energy attracts, and likely, you will soon find a reason to hate everyone you try getting close to.

When humans feel victimized by life and hold onto this emotional energy, they then attract other people into their lives who also are victims. By feeding off each other's emotional energy, they eventually become one another's victims. This is the law of universal attraction in action.

Some people feel it is easier to forgive another person for a wrongdoing than it is to forgive their self. Others find it easier to forgive their self. True emotional healing can take place only when we are willing to forgive both the other and ourselves. We must not simply tell ourselves that we forgive; we must know that we have forgiven through the balance in our feelings.

True forgiveness does not come easily and may take time. You will know when you have truly forgiven. When you can search your heart and your mind and no longer experience ill feelings toward a situation or another person, you have reached the pinnacle of true forgiving.

Following are exercises to aid you with forgiveness processing. You may do these exercises while sitting in a chair or lying in bed at night before going to sleep. These exercises should be used daily if possible.

Exercise I: *Life Revue*

While lying in bed at night, begin to revue your life. Start at the age you are now and continue back one year at a time. Say your age as you do this (such as 49) and simply see what memories come. When you come to a memory about yourself that does not feel good, it is time to process with forgiving. Simply allow yourself to receive clearly the image of what the situation was about and begin to forgive yourself for the feelings in the situation. Then see if you can understand how to forgive the other person or people involved.

When no more memories come for that year, go back one more year (e.g., age 48), and so forth. You do not have to do your entire life in one sitting. You can stop and pick up later where you left off. When you stop the first session, write down the age at which you stopped. When you do the *Life Revue* exercise again, begin at the age where you previously stopped. This exercise may take many nights or days to work with. So, be patient.

Exercise II: *The Sacred Path*

Put on some soothing, relaxing music and start letting go of all your daily stress. Feel the stress moving down your body, starting at the top of your head and moving down out through your arms and hands, then down your torso and legs, and out through your feet. Begin to drift.

Breathing comfortably, let yourself float to a peaceful place somewhere in nature. This spot is filled with greenery and earth's beauty. Spend a few moments enjoying your new surroundings, and see a traveler guiding you to a pathway. Travel this pathway and meet yourself as a child. Be gentle with yourself and the child. Let the child part of yourself express its feelings to you. Get the child to forgive you and you him/her. Forgive yourself as well. Together, recall the memories of the past that need to be resolved and work to resolve them together.

This exercise should be done many, many times. You will find that forgiveness is not an easy task to accomplish. Keep at it until you feel you are making headway and understand the process. Do not be afraid to pray or ask for help as you work on yourself.

Exercise III: *Sacred Path continued*

Use the same format of the sacred path:

After reaching your place in nature, follow your pathway with your child-self, meeting the others in your life with whom you need to do forgiveness work. Converse with each person you meet until you come to a place of forgiveness in your heart.

In doing this exercise, you will discover the many layers of feelings you need to work through.

Forgiveness is an amazing tool, that should be implemented daily.

Another example exercise:

When finding yourselves in a situation at work or home where someone is getting on your nerves; you say to yourself:

"I forgive myself for attaching to energies that are not mine. I forgive this person for being who she is."

You can choose whether to make a problem yours or not. Others energies are always around you. With forgiveness, their energies no longer influence you adversely.

If you do this exercise and the person or circumstance still bothers you, perhaps the situation is triggering an emotional response within that you need to examine.

Say to yourself,

"This person is getting on my nerves. This brings up a feeling of (*frustration* or *confusion* or *anger* or *intimidation*)."

These feelings within you are yours, even though the other person is the catalyst.

Now you say,

"I forgive myself for feeling (whatever the feeling is), and I release and let go of this feeling within me."

You will achieve the desired results only through continuous use of these exercises.

Exercise IV: *Intensive Re-patterning*

This is a chakra exercise that will help you to clear any unwanted pattern from your auric field. Set aside twenty minutes and sit for the exercise. As you begin to observe your behaviors, you will discover patterns that you really wish to change. Take one pattern at a time, and remove it from each of your chakras.

For example, an accepted pattern might be pain and suffering. Think about how pain and suffering make you feel. Then close your eyes and say:

"I forgive myself for accepting the belief pattern of pain and suffering. I release this pattern from within my soul self.

"I forgive myself for accepting the belief pattern of pain and suffering. I release this pattern from within my root chakra and physical self.

"I forgive myself for accepting the belief pattern of pain and suffering. I release this pattern from within my sacral chakra and emotional self.

"I forgive myself for accepting the belief pattern of pain and suffering. I release this pattern from within my solar plexus and mental self.

"I forgive myself for accepting the belief pattern of pain and suffering. I release this pattern from within my heart chakra and astral self.

"I forgive myself for accepting the belief pattern of pain and suffering. I release this pattern from within my throat chakra and causal self.

"I forgive myself for accepting the belief pattern of pain and suffering. I release this pattern from within my brow chakra and celestial self.

"I forgive myself for accepting the belief pattern of pain and suffering. I release this pattern from within my crown chakra and godself."

Choose any pattern that you feel is keeping you from feeling confidant. For most people, the patterns are guilt, shame, insecurity, victimization, sadness, anger, resentment, and so on. This exercise will help bring you into balance with your emotions.

Remember there is no greater tool for healing than forgiveness. When we are able to forgive, we are able to love ourselves truly. Love is the ultimate achievement in a person's life. When we become love, we attract love to us and we become loved.

Forgiveness

Write the names of all the people in your life whom you feel you need to forgive.

Write the names of all the people in your life whose forgiveness you desire.

Write what you feel you need to forgive yourself for.

Journal regularly the results of your forgiveness processing.

Affirmations

To affirm something is to make it so!

Affirmations are fun to work with. As we reprogram our emotional body it is also important to reprogram the rational mind. Our mind is a very powerful tool and we should learn to use it to our full advantage.

I equate the mind to a computer, filled with stored data containing all our past experiences and learned responses. By doing affirmations regularly, we begin storing new information in our mind that we can utilize throughout our life. Affirmations are the new program we wish to instill to work with the forgiveness and integration process. Affirmations help us empower our selves through positive self-suggestion.

We write and state our affirmations in the immediate *now* rather than in future tense. For example, "I *am* happy", "*I am fulfilled*", rather than "I will be happy" or "I will be fulfilled". This way of speaking and thinking them, acknowledges an action that is taking place now. We are placing a new energy in our force field with our affirmations while also re-programming our thinking.

When we use affirmations, we not only create a new recording for the logical mind but also create a new vibration for ourselves. Remember as spirit, we are always vibrational energy, and energy is what creates. By using affirmations, you can become a conscious creator of your empowered Self.

State your affirmations with fervor allowing your self to accept them as truth. Feel them as you state them, experience the new energy they help you produce. Deep inside, feel the feeling of what these statements reflect internally. Open yourself and allow the new energy and empowerment to emerge. The more often you repeat your affirmations, the more energy you produce for your desired achievement.

You can state affirmations aloud or simply in your mind. It is important to say them often. By writing down your affirmations and putting them in several places where you can see them constantly, such as the bathroom mirror, on your car's dashboard, as a bookmark, you will be reminded to say them daily. Doing them in this way, you will find they become constant companions and daily mantras. They can be stated anytime you have an extra moment, while combing your hair, driving your car, during television commercials, at work during breaks, or lying in bed.

Choose a set of affirmations to use and repeat them for a day or so. This will help you memorize them. Once those are memorized, add another set. When you feel ready to move on to different issues, simply choose new affirmations.

Suppose you are feeling restricted in your current way of life and want to feel unlimited. Try the following first set of affirmations.

Affirmations for feeling unlimited:
"I am unlimited."
"I am filled to overflowing."
"All my needs are easily met."

Affirmations for creating abundance:
"All the things I want and need come to me."
"I always have more than enough."
"My checking account is filled to overflowing."
"I am abundant."
"I create abundance in all that I say and do."
"I accept abundance."
"I am open to receiving all abundance."
"I draw abundance to myself today and every day."

Affirmations for feeling deserving:
"I am deserving."
"I am open and I accept myself as I am."
"I deserve abundance in all aspects of my life."
"Others see me as deserving."

Affirmations for success:
"I am successful."
"I create success in all that I do."
"I am filled with success."
"Success comes easily to me."
"Others see me as successful."

Affirmations for creating love in your life:
"My life is filled with love."
"I am love."
"I am loved."
"I am always open to and receiving love."
"I feel love for all life."

Affirmations for guilt and shame:
"I am free of guilt."
"I am unashamed."
"I am human."
"I accept all of my emotions as being good."

"I accept my guilt as good."
"I accept my shame as good."

Affirmations for joy and happiness:
"I am joyous."
"I am happy."
"All things in my life bring great joy and Happiness."
"Joy and happiness are who I am."
"I accept joy and happiness as who I am."

Affirmations for fulfillment:
"I am fulfilled."
"All things in my life bring me fulfillment."
"I am filled to overflowing."
"Fulfillment is who I am."
"I am forever filled with beauty and joy."

Affirmations for connecting to the God-self:
"I am God within."
"God and I are one."
"I am a child of God."
"I am God."

Affirmations for connecting to my light:
"I am the light within."
"I am the light of all life."
"I am a shining beacon of light."
"I am a divine emanation of light."

Affirmations for connecting to your spiritual essence:
"I am spirit."
"I am the spiritual essence of life."
"Spirit and I are one."
"All things in life are spirit."

To explore affirmations to their fullest, compose and use some of your own. Affirmations can be fun as well as useful. This new form of *self-talk* can help us with learning about self-love and self-acceptance. When we love and accept ourselves, we feel happy and prepared to live life to its fullest.

CREATE YOUR OWN AFFIRMATIONS

It is important to participate in our self-work by creating and developing our own healing tools. There will be plenty of circumstances in our life that will demand their own set of affirmations. This space is provided for you to write and record them.

1.

2.

3.

1.

2.

3.

1.

2.

3.

1.

2.

3.

1.

2.

3.

SELF-DIALOGUE

In order to truly understand ourselves we must realize that the whole is only as great as the sum of its parts. In metaphysics, these parts of the self are called aspects. We must experience ourselves as being multi-aspected and respect the process of these aspects working together to make the whole. Because we have many parts to our whole self, we need to discover and communicate with our many aspects to find inner harmony.

I call this process self-dialogue.

As we open to new ways of thinking and seeing, we develop the ability to observe our aspects. We find parts of us that are more developed than others. Our spiritual aspects are wise and loving, compassionate and understanding. Our emotional aspects are younger, less developed, and often damaged by the many incarnations in lower consciousness that have made up our lifetimes.

When we are stuck emotionally at a certain stage of growth, the stuck aspect holds back the development of the whole. This causes people to feel blocked, unable to reach specific goals.

Let me give an example:

Suppose you experienced sexual, verbal, or physical abuse as a child. You now feel that you have discovered your spiritual essence and are taking steps to live it. You try to apply the universal principles to your life, but feel blocked and do not understand why. This situation is signaling that, your repressed emotions from the past need to be explored and healed.

As children, we are not emotionally developed enough to survive abuse, and thereby separate ourselves from our feelings by repressing them. As an adult, we have the ability to look at our emotional memories and come to terms with them. This we can accomplish with self-dialog. This we do by directly communicating with the various wounded aspects of us, helping them to heal and evolve.

We dialogue with ourselves all the time. Most of our self-dialogue is destructive rather than constructive. Generally, we beat ourselves up by criticizing our every thought and action. We developed this pattern at a very early stage of life. The first aspect of yourself that you may wish to address is this critical part.

Self-dialogue Exercise I

Sit or lie in a comfortable position and begin to relax. Use these affirmations: "I relax. I am relaxing even more. I feel deeply relaxed."

Say these affirmations continuously while breathing calmly for about three minutes. Begin feeling yourself drift and allow the feeling of criticism to begin emerging. Welcome the feeling by saying, "I welcome the part of myself that feels critical. I ask that you please come up within me at this time and show yourself to me so I can speak with you directly."

When this aspect within you begins to surface, you may experience a sensation of a person or actually get a picture. You may simply see a mirror-like reflection of yourself or you may encounter a person who seems ugly or angry. You may simply have a feeling come up.

It matters not how your aspect appears. What matters is your communication with this part of yourself. Ask the aspect why s/he feels the need to be so critical. Listen to what the aspect tells you. Dialogue with the aspect at length. Let this part of yourself know that you agree with the reasons s/he gives for the feelings. Tell the aspect that you understand and accept his/her reasons for feeling critical. Tell this part of yourself that you honor her/him and the role s/he plays in your life. Let it know that whatever occurred to make her/him feel this way was a misguided teaching and the reason you are communicating with this aspect now is to correct and change that understanding. Allow your inner wisdom to help you explain how damaging it is to both of you to be so critical. Let the aspect know that you need and want his/her help and agreement in order to change this pattern between you. Open your heart and offer the aspect the love s/he needs in order to feel differently. Let the aspect know that through the love you both now share everything can change and heal. Feel this part of yourself coming into your heart and accepting the love you offer. Feel the integration take place.

Self-dialogue Exercise II

Imagine that you are up for a promotion and you feel obsessively stressed and worried. Begin the same way with this exercise as for the one above. Use your relaxation affirmations: "I relax. I am relaxing even more. I feel deeply relaxed."

While breathing calmly, say the relaxation affirmations over and over for about three minutes. Then say, "I now welcome the part of myself that feels obsessed and worried. I open myself to you and ask you please to come up within me so I can speak with you directly."

Allow yourself to feel this aspect moving up into your awareness. Again, you may see a mirror-like reflection of yourself or you may simply feel this emotion. You may encounter a very angry person, a haggard person, a forlorn person, or perhaps a young person. What matters is *how* you communicate with this aspect of yourself.

Ask the aspect what s/he is trying to teach you and what s/he wants and needs from you. This aspect of yourself is missing something very important, and you are the only one who can address and fill its needs. Listen to the aspect and acknowledge his/her feelings. Take the time to hear this part of yourself. This aspect is probably a strong part of you. As you listen, you will begin to understand and see that what the aspect is saying has truth.

Now call upon your inner wisdom to help you explain to this part of yourself why it no longer needs to stay stuck in this way of feeling. Do this by sharing a new perspective with this aspect of your self. Always, be kind and understanding as you do this.

For example, this aspect may begin sharing experiences from your past in which you felt you were "burned" every time you trusted in yourself or someone else. Feel the feelings involved with those past experiences, but also understand that you no longer choose to dwell in that reality.

Now share with the aspect that, yes indeed, that was true in the past; however, that if the aspect will trust you now, together you can create a new method for handling such situations that will bring happiness and fulfillment.

During this exercise, you may encounter mistrust and resistance from an aspect. In this circumstance, you may have to find a more creative way of convincing a part of yourself that what you propose is in the best interest of the whole; this may take some time.

With this process, you may find that an aspect integrates temporarily but has a tendency to fragment again at different stages of your development. Do not be discouraged if this occurs, simply keep working at the integration. The results that come from this process are long-term and profound. You can truly integrate the fragments of yourself and free yourself emotionally. You will begin to believe in yourself and your life again. This occurs as you integrate and heal into the whole person that you are.

Just as in our biological families, each of us is a family within ourselves, we have members who are older and wiser, younger, still growing, parents, and so on. When all the members of your inner family acknowledge and accept one another, you are in harmony. When the members of your inner family are at odds, your life is filled with obstacles that make you uncomfortable and unhappy.

The aspects that comprise your inner family are your spirit essence, spiritual guides and teachers of light, as well as your physical experience aspects. We must learn to address and understand all of our aspects to attain inner harmony. By acknowledging and communing with them, in the manner put forth, you can heal into your whole self. In this way, you become your own teacher and your own best friend.

Your aspects are well versed in all the areas of self-learning and personal expansion. Integration allows your whole being to function harmoniously in both the spiritual and physical worlds. Integration brings us the understanding of heaven on earth.

Self-Dialogue Exercises

1. Ask yourself, "What am I afraid to talk to myself about?" Write down everything that comes to mind. Read it aloud and dialogue with yourself about it.

2. Ask yourself, "How many people or personalities live inside me?" Speak to each aspect individually, just as you would with any person. Keep a journal of the work you do with each aspect of yourself. You may find that you have given a feeling—such as guilt or shame—a personality. That is okay!

Visualization: *A Key to Awareness*

Visualization, or imagery, is a wonderful tool for enlightenment! Regular practice, opens us to the many dimensions within, and can have profound effects in our physical recall and body awareness.

Some people think visualization or using imagination to be a waste of time. They think using imagination is childish and a lot of nonsense. These individuals have forgotten how to play and create newness in their life. Life is built on the use of imagination, without it, there would be no inventions or discovery. Using creative imagination allows us to freely experience the different dimensions of our self and the universe.

Visualization operates with feelings. At first, you may see nothing at all but you may feel a great deal. If you are trying to visualize something and can feel different things within yourself, you are experiencing the desired effect. Learning to interpret what you are feeling will help you understand your inner self. This opens your perception and helps you see a much broader picture of yourself and life as a whole.

Each of us is different so our reported experiences will be different as well. Do not be concerned with how other people visualize, simply find a method that works best for you. Visualizing helps you to let go of what you think you believe so you can explore the unknown realms of consciousness. Here you can learn to see, think, and feel conceptually. The more you practice visualizing, the more proficient you will become.

Visualizing can be great fun a whole new dimension of self, just waiting to be explored! Are you an explorer? Have you wondered what is contained in your soul's memory? Do you want to see into the inner worlds to know if they really exist? If so – Visualization can take you there.

Visualization helps us unlock our inner vision. Do not worry about whether you are making it up. Imagination puts us in touch with our creativity.

Exercise I: Becoming *the Light*

Sit in a chair with your feet flat on the floor and your back straight. Repeat the mantra, "I am that I am... I am that I am... I am that I am."

Breathe evenly and slowly, repeating, "I am relaxed... I am more deeply relaxed... I am fully relaxed."

Continue saying these mantras over and over until you feel relaxed.

Now visualize the sun shining directly overhead. Feel its radiance and brightness surrounding you. Feel its penetrating warmth while you experience its golden rainbow of colors, yellow, reds, oranges, and shimmering multicolored light.

Allow yourself to be pulled closer and closer to the bright light until you merge and become one with it. Expand yourself out as the light into every different direction imaginable.

Exercise II: You *Are the Ocean*

Sit or lie comfortably. Breathing evenly and slowly, say, "I am the light within... I am that I am... I am the light within... I am relaxed... I am more deeply relaxed... I am fully relaxed."

Do this continuously until you feel yourself relaxing.

Feel yourself begin floating upon the ocean. Let the salt water hold you up as the waves lap all around you. Feel the spray of the water on your face. Smell the sea salt air. Feel the rocking motion of the water as it moves you back and forth. See the clouds in the sky above. Close your eyes in the visualization and relax into everything around you, allowing yourself to become one with the water. Feel the awe of how great and powerful the feeling experience is. Lose yourself in the experience by simply letting go and becoming the ocean.

Exercise III: *A Journey into Consciousness*

Sit in a chair, or lie down. Concentrate on your breathing. Use your mantra: "I am the light within... I am the light... I am relaxed... I am completely relaxed... I am fully relaxed."

Feel yourself becoming lighter, and lighter and lighter until you are weightless, now effortlessly floating like a feather, allow the airwaves to carry you.

Allow the air currents to gently carry you out through a window. Feel the freeing sensation of floating on a breeze without a care in the world. As you look down you see yourself crossing over the ocean and see a white sparkling beach ahead. Effortlessly you are transported by the breeze to its beautiful, glimmering sands.

Notice the breath-taking beauty all around. Look down at your feet, see them bare and melding into the soft sand. Notice all the different varieties of plants and flowers. Smell the aromas. Notice the colors of all the life around you, the water, the trees, the rocks or cliffs.

Coming down the beach toward you is a beautiful winged horse. It invites you to mount and fly above this beautiful terrain. From above, the view is breathtaking. Magically you fly higher and higher, up past the clouds and into the blue sky.

You can see a castle in the distance and your winged horse flies towards it. You arrive at the castle finding it to have two beautifully ornate doors. As you stand before them, you experience a strong feeling of familiarity. You have a sense of being here before, so you open the doors and enter.

Inside is a marble floor, a staircase on the left, and hallways on the right. In the center of this grand entry is a fountain with a real mermaid. You discover you feel very comfortable being in her presence. You actually feel quite safe and realize that the two of you are able to commune with each other without speaking. This makes you feel joyous as you remember that you are actually a part of all life. You bask in this feeling for a while and then find yourself-drawn to the hallway on the right. As you explore, you discover a ballroom, a banquet room, sitting rooms, and a library. Some of these rooms are filled with people, while others contain only furnishings.

You are now drawn to go back to the entry and climb the staircase. Allowing your intuition to guide you, you discover a special room. You enter.

Your sensations tell you that you have been in this room before. Everything feels quite familiar and the decor reminds you of yourself in some way. You explore the room to see if there are hidden memories you may have left here. Memories of another time or place perhaps. You look to see if there is a child or other person waiting for you, ready to help you explore.

Exercise IV: *Healing Your Chakras and Subtle Bodies*

Take a few minutes to center. Concentrate on your breathing. Or use a mantra, such as, *"I am light... I am the God within... I am light... I am relaxed... I am completely relaxed... I am fully relaxed. Say this over and over until you feel relaxed.*

Etheric body. Once you are relaxed and centered, move your attention to your root chakra at the base of your spine. See the color red pouring through this vortex of spiraling energy.

Now, see blue webbing connected to the chakra, expanding out and surrounding the body, eight to ten feet.

Begin looking for rips or tears in the blue webbing. Direct a blue laser light from the center of your hand to seal and heal any rips or tears you find. Now seal the outside of the webbing with a silvery liquid fluid for reinforcement.

Command that this healed etheric subtle body be in balance and harmony with the physical self.

Emotional body. Now move to your sacral chakra. See its vortex energy filled with a vibrant orange color. Now see a pastel cloud connected to the chakra. Expand the cloud out eight to ten feet.

Look closely to see if the colors are bright and clear or murky and dull. Mentally use the *Forgiveness Process* to heal any black or murky areas in the body; eliminate any stubborn areas that do not brighten.

Once you feel you have healed the emotional body, ask that it be in balance and harmony with the physical self.

Mental body. Feel yourself move up into the solar plexus, one inch above the navel. See this vortex spiral filled with a vibrant yellow color. See golden rays extending outward from it. Make sure all of the rays are straight. Ask that the mental body be in balance and harmony with the physical self.

Astral body. Now move to the heart chakra. See this vortex energy center filled with a vibrant green color. See the astral body connected to it as almost transparent. Expand the astral body out eight to ten feet. If this body is murky or has black spots, clear it until it is transparent. Ask that the astral body be in balance and harmony with the physical self.

Causal body. Now move to the throat chakra. See this vortex energy center filled with a beautiful ice-blue color. See the causal body connected to it, as a blueprint of you. Here you can change any and all illnesses, habits, and misalignments. Now feel the causal body come into you, so you can experience the changes you have created.

Celestial body. Now move to the brow chakra. See this energy center filled with a deep indigo color. See the celestial body connected to it as a collage of beautiful multi-colored glittering lights. Expand the celestial body and enjoy the energy it brings to you. Ask that this body be aligned with your other bodies.

Ketheric body. Now move to the chakra center at the crown of the head. The ketheric body is a golden orb of light, known as the God body or Christ self. This body encases all the other bodies within it, including the physical body. Let yourself enjoy the soothing vibration and healing energy of the wonderful spiritual gold of the God body.

Visualization Goals

1. Journal what you felt or saw during your visualizations.

2. Create and write out your own visualizations.

3. Explore guided meditation and guided visualization tapes. Record your own.

About the Author

Athene Raefiel began having visions of other realms at the young age of ten. At twenty-eight, she began searching for the meaning of spirituality. Through meditation and meditative trance practices, she began ongoing spirit communication with Angels and Teachers of Light. At age thirty-eight she received personal visitations from Archangels Michael, Raphael, Gabriel and Uriel. She also received personal visitations from Ascended masters St. Germain, Lord Meitreya and Morya El.

She spent three years traveling into different dimensions of learning where she received spiritual teachings and dissertations from a number of different master teachers.

She had her first experience of being taken into the light when she was thirty-three and has experienced visions her entire life.

Athene spent many years studying comparative religions and finding the thread of truth that runs through all spiritual teachings. Eastern philosophies, such as Buddhism, Brahman, and Hinduism, brought her into an awareness of pure metaphysics, the science of the soul.

In 1984, Athene began teaching classes on connecting with Spirit Guides, Angels, and Teachers of Light. She also taught classes on dreams, inner-child work, channeling, numerology, astrology, and guided imagery. She is a teacher of mysticism and enlightenment.

Athene Raefiel has conducted professional, intuitive counseling and transformative healing treatments since 1986. She received her Clinical Hypnotherapist Certification (CCHT) in 1996 from the Transpersonal Hypnotherapy Institute in Boulder, Colorado. She completed intensive Mediation training with CDR Associates in Boulder Co. in 2001.

Athene has hosted her own radio shows in Rhode Island, Connecticut, Arizona. She has been Lecturing at Holistic Fairs since 1986 and continues to write articles that are published in a variety of metaphysical magazines and websites.

**To contact Athene Raefiel, go to
www.atheneraefiel.com**

Suggested Reading

On Chakras:
The Truth About Chakras, Anodea Judith
The Awakening of Kundalini, Gopi Krishna
Introduction to the Chakras, Peter Rendel
Working with Your Chakras, Ruth White
Esoteric Healing, Alice A. Bailey
Hands of Light, Barbara A. Brennan

On Affirmations:
Books by Stuart Wilde, Shakti Gawain, and Louise Hay

Soul Consciousness:
Seat of the Soul by Gary Zukov

Authors of Interest:
H. P. Blavatsky
C.W. Leadbetter
Alice Baily
Deepak Chopra
Carolyn Myss

GLOSSARY

Taken from "Occult Glossary" By: G. de PURUCKER
Theosophical University Press: Pasadena, California

Akashic. From Sanskrit Akasa. The word means "brilliant," "shining," "luminous." The fifth cosmic element, the fifth essence or "quintessence", called Aether by the ancient stoics. It is also Mulaprakriti, the cosmical spirit substance, the reservoir of Being and of beings.

Ascension. The passage of life-waves or life-streams evolving upwards. The ascent from the physical to the spiritual.

Aspect. The appearance of an object of thought as viewed by the mind.

Astral. The invisible region surrounding our earth. A cosmic picture gallery or indelible record of whatever takes place on the astral and physical planes.

Aura. A subtle and invisible essence that emanates from and surrounds not only human beings and animals, but plants and minerals as well. It is an electric magnetic field, suffused with the energies of mind and spirit. It is the source of the sympathies and antipathies that we are conscious of. Under the control of the human will, it can be either life giving and healing, or death dealing. When the human will is passive, the aura has an action of its own which is automatic and follows the laws of character and latent impulses of the being from which it emanates.

Auric Egg. It is the source of the human aura as well as everything else that the human septenary constitution contains. It ranges from the divine to the astral-physical, and is the seat of all the monadic, spiritual, intellectual, mental, passional, and vital energies and faculties of the human septiform constitution.

Awareness. Knowing something either by perception or by a means of information.

Buddhism. The teachings of Gautama the Buddha. Buddhism today is divided into two branches, the Northern and the Southern. The Southern retains the teachings of "Buddha's Brain" the "Eye Doctrine," or his outer philosophy for the outer world. The Northern retains his "Heart Doctrine"---that which is hidden, the inner life or heart blood of the religion: the doctrine of the inner heart teaching.

Causal Body. Causal Plane. The causal body is sometimes known as the soul. This causal body and causal plane are what determines the cycle of re-incarnations a being does experience. It is no *body* at all but rather the essence of new manifestations or re-embodiment. The causal plane is the plane of cause and effect.

Chakra. A word signifying wheel. Chakra also means a cycle in which the wheel of time turns once.

Clairaudience. True clairaudience is a spiritual faculty of the inner spiritual ear. The power to hear with the inner ear enables you to hear anything you will, no matter what the distance, but is most useful when used to hear into the various dimensions of spirit-self.

Clairvoyance. The ability to see beyond the veil of illusion into the truth of light and oneness of self and soul. You see clearly with your eyes closed and well beyond the physical dimension.

Conceptualism. That universals, or abstract concepts, exist only within the mind and have no external reality.

Consciousness. Consciousness is spirit matter. Force and matter, or spirit and substance, are one – hence consciousness is the finest form of energy, is the root of all things, and is co-extensive with cosmic space.

Dimension. A measure of spatial extent, magnitude, size.

Energetic. The physics of energy and its transformations.

Enlighten. To give knowledge or truth to; endow with spiritual understanding.

Essence. The inherent, unchanging nature of a thing or class of things.

Evolution. Bringing forth of what is within. Growth, unfolding of faculty and organ, unwrapping of latent powers native to the entity itself.

Experience. Apprehension of an object, thought, or emotion through the senses or mind.

Guides. Those who show the way by leading or advising, by reason of their greater experience with the course to be pursued.

Illumination. Spiritual enlightenment.

Meditate. To reflect upon, ponder or contemplate.

Metaphysics. The branch of philosophy that systematically investigates the nature of first principles and problems of ultimate reality. The science of the soul.

Oversoul. A spiritual essence or vital force in the universe, in which all souls participate.
Transcends individual consciousness.

The Path. Universal nature exists inseparably in each one of us. The pathway is within yourselves. There is no other pathway for you individually than the pathway leading ever inwards towards your own inner god.

Planes. The various range or steps of the hierarchical ladder of lives that melt and blend into each other. The physical world grades off into the astral world, which grades off again into a world higher than it, the world which is superior to the astral world; and so it continues throughout the series of hierarchical steps which compose a universe such as ours.

Refract. To deflect light.

Reincarnation. The soul returning to a specific place to take on a specific embodiment a second, third, or any number of times.

Repression. To hold inside or within oneself.

Self. A purely spiritual unit, in its essence divine, which is the same in every man and woman on earth. The same in every entity everywhere in all the boundless fields of limitless space.

Soul. The soul is the vehicle used to work out our destiny. A "soul" is an entity which is evolved by experiences; it is not a spirit but a vehicle of a spirit. On the higher planes the "soul" is a vehicle manifesting as a sheaf or pillar of light. This light is carried down into matter by the bearer all the way into the physical body.

Source. Point of origin.

Spirit. Our immortal element. The deathless flame within us which never dies, which never was born, and which retains throughout all cycles its own quality, essence, and life sending to us and into our various planes certain of its rays or garments which we are.

Trance. A state of detachment from ones physical surroundings, as in contemplation or daydreaming. A state between waking and sleeping.

Transmute. To change from one form or state into another.

Truth. Reality; actuality. To realize and actualize reality through all levels of consciousness within and without.

Unconditional. Without limitations or conditions.

www.ingramcontent.com/pod-product-compliance
Lightning Source LLC
Chambersburg PA
CBHW030117100526
44591CB00009B/435